AUTHENTIC
MISSION

AUTHENTIC MISSION

Authentic Mission is a unique expression of Mission in the Australian context. It seeks a new direction and focus on mission work, new thinking, new undertakings and a new expression of the church towards Australian society.

Authentic Mission clearly pursues the transformation of Australian Society concurrent with a transformation of the Church.

Authentic Mission recognises an intelligent confrontation with its host secular society is necessary. Authentic Mission speaks the truth without fear, guards' Catholic rights and is prepared to face the consequences of such actions. The outcome of Authentic mission is the transformation of Australian society leading to the salvation of the individual.

AUTHENTIC

MISSION

Transforming Society Through a
Revitalized Church

Fr James Grant

Connor Court Publishing

Published in 2020 by Connor Court Publishing Pty Ltd
Copyright © Fr James Grant 2020

All rights reserved. No part of this book may be reproduced or transmitted in any form or by any means, electronic or mechanical, including photocopying, recording or by any information storage and retrieval system, without prior permission in writing from the publisher.

Connor Court Publishing Pty Ltd
PO Box 7257
Redland Bay QLD 4165

sales@connorcourt.com
www.connorcourtpublishing.com.au
Phone 0497 900 685

ISBN: 9781922449016
Front Cover Design: Brad Ashlock
Printed in Australia

ACKNOWLEDGEMENTS

In remembrance of the life and mission of
Fr Bernhard Lichtenberg (1875 – 1943)
Opponent of National Socialism and
defender of the Catholic faith
A witness without fear

Stephanie Mignanelli
In gratefulness for her hard work and
patience

With special thanks to Belinda and Debra
Carroll for their ongoing support and
fundraising

With special thanks to Brad Ashlock
cover design and graphics
Enquiries: bradashlock@gmail.com

ABOUT THE AUTHOR

Fr James Grant MAICD BA BTh GDip IS GDip Comp ST GDip Trauma Counselling.

Born in Adelaide, and schooled in Essendon, Victoria. Fr James joined the Commonwealth Police in 1977 with an initial posting in Canberra. He has qualified as a martial arts instructor in Brazilian Jiu Jitsu, scuba diving and played first grade cricket for Northcote.

Fr James undertook theological studies at Melbourne University, graduating in 1984. Appointed to the UK as an associate priest, he became one of London's first white vicars to minister to the expanding West Indian community. Fr James initiated his first interfaith gatherings in west London following the Brixton riots, after which he was appointed on short term placement to Berlin (West Germany) in 1988 and Budapest in 1989.

Fr James returned to Australia in 1989 where he was Senior Chaplain at Geelong Grammar School for seven years, followed by two years at St Michael's grammar and six years at The Peninsula School. He was noted for his pastoral care with a focus on martial arts, football and cricket as methods for building confidence in students.

In 2004 he was appointed a parish priest at St Stephen's Richmond, then in 2005 Melbourne's first team vicar for the new parish of Jika Jika in Melbourne's north with responsibility for a large Sudanese refugee community. As Parish priest for the Preston area, he was a strong advocate for the Nuba people, of Sudan, who are experiencing genocide. He has built two schools in Northern India.

Fr James founded Chaplains Without Borders in 2004 to initiate new ventures into corporate and community organisations, and CWB grew to be Australia's largest chaplaincy service within 2 years. He went on to be appointed as the world's first chaplain to the casino industry in 2006 (Crown Resorts).

As a leading traditionalist within the Australian church, Fr James supported the development to the Anglican Ordinariate in Australia and served on the national committee as secretary 2010-2011. Fr James was received into the Catholic Church and ordained as a Catholic Priest in September 2012.

He is the first Chaplain appointed to an A league soccer club in Australia at the largest Australian club, Melbourne Victory. He is involved with 9MM and 45ACP pistol and rifle competition and is completing PPLH training.

In 2013 Fr James established the Father James Grant Foundation, implementing programs for de-motivated young Australians. The "Mission Engage "program has now helped around 800 young Australians find their first Job.

Web

www.chaplainswithoutborders.org

www.catholicsengaged.com

www.missionengageyouth.org

BY THE SAME AUTHOR

Resurgence – Revitalising Western Catholicism

Let There Be Light – Parish Leadership for the 21st Century

Keeping The Faith – The Battle for Australian Catholicism

How Not to be A Victim – Vital challenges from the mission engage program

FOREWORDS

John Roskam

Authentic Mission by Fr James Grant is a brilliant, provocative, and absolutely necessary work.

With searing clarity Fr James analyses the failures and problems of the Catholic Church in Australia, but with clear-eyed and relentless optimism he charts a course for the Church into the future. That future is centred on the idea of 'mission'. *Authentic Mission – Transforming Society Through a Revitalized Church* challenges the Church as a whole, and every Catholic as an individual to engage in the world and not to retreat from it.

As Fr James puts it so beautifully – 'Underlying mission is the critical idea that mission is Catholic culture in action, mission is what you do, but you are not 'selling' program, services, bible studies or anything else. Mission involving 'living' and expressing your Catholic culture and values.

Expressed in this way 'mission' is a radical idea. It requires the unapologetic expression of explicitly *Catholic* culture and values. And mission that's relevant to all Australians requires the expression of ideals that are within the mainstream of this country's culture and values. As Fr James writes so passionately about, a commitment to for example the dignity of work, or the notion of Australia as overwhelmingly a fair and tolerant nation must be part of the mission of the Catholic Church in this country.

There would not be a Catholic priest in Australia who has a better understanding of the current condition of young people. As Fr James accurately describes it, there is a 'Generation Adrift':

> They are a generation severely affected by depression, they have extensive issues in transitioning to work, often have no concept of what they hope for from life, are often disconnected from parents and family, and many are enthralled to a life of illicit drugs.

The Church's mission to young people requires helping provide a sense of meaning and vocation to this generation that is adrift. As Fr James acutely observes a sense of purpose will not derive from 'the gimmicks of apps, rock masses and dance performance.'

The American Catholic writer and historian, George Weigel recently commented that when the Catholic Church is best at bearing witness when it understands the truth about itself as an 'evangelical, missionary enterprise' that carries a social doctrine that helps make sense of the incoherence of the world around it.

'Making sense of incoherence' – especially the incoherence of the postmodern world – might at first sight sound strange as part of the purpose of the mission of the Church – but to know where we want to go and what we want to be it is first necessary to know where we are and what we are. And this is true whether we are talking about an institution such as the Catholic Church, or about ourselves as individuals, or our families or our communities.

Only a sense of mission can help us make sense of incoherence. *Authentic Mission* is grounded in Christ's words – *For God did not send his Son into the world to condemn the world but the save the world through him.*

David Robarts OAM

I am fortunate to have been closely associated with Father James Grant in a variety of Church related projects and initiatives over some 20 years. His many years of varied experience as priest/ educator also continue to find expression as an innovative entrepreneur through such initiatives as his "Chaplains without Borders", and the "Father James Grant Foundation" – which amongst other things, provides windows of hope and programmes of opportunity for unemployed youth. He is both a man of ideas and also practical application. What brings all this together is his deep Faith in Christ and passionate longing for the Church to recover its vocation and motivation to embody Christ's dynamic Mission to transform the world. His is a truly prophetic and fearless voice that needs to be heard in today's media drenched wilderness of confused and confusing opinions.

This is a most important book, for it is a wake-up call to a Church which has largely lost its identity, succumbing to secular agendas rather than that of Jesus Christ. It is now a seriously compromised Church, lacking a voice to be heard in the Market Place, or provide leadership in matters of Catholic principle for its people. Nowhere is this clearer than in that most fundamental of reasons for her existence – its Mission – which has been largely "outsourced" to organisations, programmes, and top-down talkfests, rather than embraced and lived by Christian Communities themselves. Jesus commits his mission to us in our baptism, by making us part of His new Creation. We become His hands and feet for Mission; He has no other. In the words of Reinhold Niebuhr: "the Church exists for Mission as a Fire does for burning".

Back in the 1960's I attended an important International Conference attended by many Church leaders and representatives of Missionary Organizations. It was clear that all was not well with regard to Church Missionary endeavour. The most impressive contributor was a youngish but very able priest with a passion for Mission. He upset a number of people, particularly those with an investment in the status quo. He kept reminding us that the Church was not geared to Mission but Maintenance. This became a common complaint; indeed, it is still with us, only things have progressively deteriorated. Parishes amalgamate and decline, priests are overburdened; working in an environment of survival mode is demoralizing and robs people of hope. What then is to be done?

The earlier chapters of this book open to us a variety of models which are unlikely to be fruitful: the spiritual and inward looking; the church as club; the therapeutic church, the programmed Church. Catholic emphasis on social justice issues is strong – indigenous affairs, refugees, increased welfare, climate change. However, these are not largely pertinent to the life of the parishes themselves. How is the parish itself and its people to engage in what Father James calls Authentic Mission? He says: "Mission is an action of choosing to 'live' and 'to be' the faith with all the cost that entails. It is a concrete decision for Christ." Such Catholic Mission is a local activity, it is painful and costly but also energizing and transforming.

The latter part of the book sets before us an astonishing range of possibilities for transformation that may renew Christian life and witness at the local level. He sees the Parish as a place of healing for the young who are adrift, the drug affected, single parents, the disadvantaged and the burdened.

This is a challenging and remarkable book, full of hope for the hopeless, for those hungry for a Gospel to live by, and be inspired by Jesus and His Saints. Like myself, Father James has a deep and enduring concern for the Persecuted Church and the inspiration of its martyrs, so neglected by a largely indifferent West.

A final missiological thought from Thomas Merton the day before he died in 1968. "What we are now asked to do is not so much speak of Christ as to let Him live within us, so that people may feel him by the way He is living in us."

Morgan Begg

Civil society organisations such as churches will be immensely important institutions in the period following the 2020 COVID-19 pandemic. The ramifications of the economic lockdown and compulsory social isolation measures across Australia in response to the virus are not fully known but it is probable that the economy will not simply be reset to a pre-pandemic status quo. In the aftermath churches will be needed to provide relief and spiritual guidance to Australian communities as they are confronted by uncommonly difficult circumstances. Are they prepared?

Aside from restrictions on social gatherings, Australian governments have also prohibited or restricted a number of businesses and recreational facilities and activities from operating as normal. The Institute of Public Affairs calculated that 717,000 jobs had been lost between 25 March 2020 and 3 April 2020 during the economic lockdown. Moreover, this was likely to be a conservative estimate as it did not include the number of jobs that had been retained but on new terms, such as reduced hours. Nor does it include the jobs that have been lost outside of that 10-day window.

The short-term goal of not letting an unknown virus spread across Australia and not overwhelm the health system is a valid policy goal, and the protection of life in Australia is always a valid goal of government. However, there is a considerable cost in terms of extended unemployment and denial of opportunity that presents and considerable mental health risk that may only be revealed fully when the virus itself no longer presents a serious public health threat.

In this context there is a massive role for Churches in communities to provide relief and spiritual counsel for an overwhelming number of Australians who will continue to struggle in a stagnating economy that will not simply turn back on at the flip of a switch. This is part and parcel of the fundamental goal of a Christian church: to engage with society to promote the good word and works of Christ and resurrect the lives of individuals not only spiritually but by directing them to adopt the habits, values and practices of a "good life", even when circumstances are unkind to them.

However, as the past books of Father James Grant have exposed, the Catholic Church, the largest single religious denomination in Australia, has failed in this fundamental goal. It is in danger of not being prepared for this role because it has failed to speak with a consistent and principled message about the values of the church and the moral message of leading a good life.

The past books of Father James Grant have focused on the problems of the Catholic Church in Australia, and its failure to represent the faith, to participate in communities as an effective social and spiritual force, while overseeing a diminishing flock, as according to most recent Census data. As Father James noted in his 2017 book, *Keeping the Faith: The Battle for Australian Catholicism*, many Australian church leaders have "become strongly attached to the ad hoc, shoot from the hip style of leadership offered by the papacy of Pope Francis.' This is also characterised by the lack of any serious leadership to present a united Church which is consistent and principled in its message and its Christian mission leading to different Catholic figures seeking the favour of media outlets which are hostile to traditional Christian thought as a path by adopting the attitudes and expressing the beliefs of the progressive secular elite.

Keeping the Faith and other writings of Father James have successfully chronicled the failure of Western church leaders. Now Father James has taken what he has learned and written about the problems of the church to craft a new path forward to revitalise Catholicism in Australia. The "Authentic Mission" as Father James has named it, means "fighting and contesting for Church values and beliefs in the public forum". This will not be an easy path for indolent church bureaucrats which are comfortable pursuing the path of least resistance – defined by diminishing church numbers and appeasing a media machine which ultimately remains a hostile force against Christianity.

It is especially timely for Father James to chart this course for Australian churches. Being at the forefront of the debate about the dignity is important at a time of extended economic stagnation we appear to be headed towards. A society that is shutdown needs something to be hopeful for, rather than the hopelessness offered by addiction and crime. Issues about the reversal of the presumption of innocence in the High Court's unanimous decision to overturn the conviction of Cardinal George Pell in March 2020 expose a deeper institutional hostility against the church and religious freedom and persecution of Christians.

In this respect Father James brings credibility and experience to the debate. His leadership of Chaplains Without Borders in 2004 to venture into corporate and community organisations became Australia's largest chaplaincy service within two years of its formation. In 2015 Father James established the Father James Grant Foundation to implement programmes for demotivated young Australians. The Mission Engage has now assisted in putting 800 young Australians find their first jobs, helping them find the dignity of work for the first time.

In my review of *Keeping the Faith* published in the *IPA Review* in May 2018, I unhesitatingly remarked that "the Catholic Church in Australia is very fortunate to have Father James in its ranks... The Vatican needs more in the mould of Father James and, frankly, less in the mould of Pope Francis." I will now take the opportunity to expand the sentiment to say that all Christians in Australia are blessed to have Father James in their column, and that while his guide for success is targeted towards the Catholic Church, all Christian denominations should heed his message rediscover their purpose and to help make Australia a safe, secure, and prosperous country.

Francis Mary Simon Chen MEngSc

Most days on my way to work in the morning, I will bump into Father Grant outside a food court at Crown Melbourne. We say our 'Hellos'. Now and then, we have a brief chat. We chat about general things: the news, current affairs, everyday stuff but sometimes, we talk about the Catholic Church. Before we know it, these talks can become serious as we pose to ourselves, some simple questions:

What does it mean to be 'Catholic'? Nowadays, we seem to get mixed messages from different bishops, priests, the religious, laity and even from those within Church hierarchy.

Why aren't Catholics attending Church regularly? In many places, the numbers attending Sunday Mass are relatively small. Less young people and young families are engaging with Catholic faith. Just, what's going on and how might it be fixed?

Learned theologians and philosophers and social science have their answers. Yet in our chats, we find ourselves circling back to something that is central to our faith.

That our purpose as Catholics is to love the Lord our God with all our heart, soul and mind. That to love Jesus is to reach out to Him as He is seen in the family of people everywhere. That we can best reach out to others when we do missionary work.

As Pope Francis puts it:

> *The Church is on mission in the world. ... A Church that presses forward to the farthest frontiers requires a constant and ongoing missionary conversion. This missionary mandate touches us personally: I am a mission, always; you are a mission, always; every baptized man and woman is a mission. ... Our mission, then, is rooted in the fatherhood of God and the motherhood of the Church. The mandate given by the Risen Jesus at Easter is inherent in Baptism: as the Father has sent me, so I send you, filled with the Holy Spirit, for the reconciliation of the world (cf. Jn 20:19-23; Mt 28:16-20). This mission is part of our identity as Christians; it makes us responsible for enabling all men and women to realise their vocation to be adoptive children of the Father, to recognize their personal dignity and to appreciate the intrinsic worth of every human life, from conception until natural death. Today's rampant secularism, when it becomes an aggressive cultural rejection of God's active fatherhood in our history, is an obstacle to authentic human fraternity, which finds expression in reciprocal respect for the life of each person.*

These ideas are the genesis for Father Grant's new book and its focus on what he calls 'Authentic Mission'.

Drawing from personal insight and from his experience in giving pastoral care to the breadth and depth of society, Authentic Mission is Father Grant's battle cry for a reawakened Catholic Church that remains true to its Christian identity.

We need to strengthen and expand our social and community ties. We need to be tied to God.

CONTENTS

INTRODUCTION – HOW ARE WE REALLY
   GOING?   27

SECTION I – THREATS AND ERRORS
(I) THE BENEDICT OPTION – ROD DREHER   33
(II) JOIN THE CLUB – The Anglican Option   39
(II.I) Will Catholicism take the Anglican Option?   44
(III) THE PROGRAMMED CHURCH   47
(IV) THE THERAPEUTIC CHURCH   58
(V) THE SOCIAL JUSTICE CHURCH   63
(VI) CLIMATE, CAPITALISM AND LOST
   SHEPHERDS   69
(VII) VATICAN SILENCE IN CHINA   74
(VIII) THE NEW SOCIALISM   81
(IX) A SOCIETY OF TRIBES   85

SECTION II – UNDERSTANDING AUTHENTIC MISSION
(I) AUTHENTIC MISSION – INTELLIGENT
   CONFRONTATION   91
(II) NO MISSION – NO LIFE   99
(III) THE ESSENTIAL DIFFERENCE OF
   AUTHENTIC THEOLOGY   106

(IV) AUTHENTIC MISSION IN ACTION	112
(V) THE ELEPHANT IN THE ROOM – WHAT DOES FATHER DO?	138

SECTION III – AUTHENTIC MISSION IN ACTION

(I) THE DIGNITY OF WORK	150
(II) SUPPORT THE DISADVANTGED AND BURDENDED	156
(III) HELP SINGLE PARENTS	166
(IV) BATTING FOR AUSTRALIA	175
(V) GENERATION ADRIFT	183
(VI) DRUGS	201
(VII) THE HEALING PARISH	212
(VIII) AFFIRM THE MARTYRS	221
(IX) SUPPORT PERSECUTED CHRISTIANS	228

APPENDIX – AUTHENTIC MISSION: IN DEPTH   237

INTRODUCTION

1. HOW ARE WE REALLY GOING?

The Australian Catholic Church mistakenly believes that if it adapts to its surrounding society and values it will be given an honoured place within Australia's community life. If life teaches us anything it should be that our hopes and expectations do not often correlate into what we believe should happen.

The Catholic Church in Australia has been in slow decline for over 40 years, yet there is little acknowledgement of this reality, despite internal church statistics and Australian government census information indicating such a decline, the church largely slumbers on as if nothing has changed.

Not only is the total number of practicing Catholics in sharp decline the number of available priests has also fallen severely, resulting in a "new normal" of merged parishes sometimes with one priest in charge of up to three centres (all formerly stand-alone parishes).

Catholic atrophy is even more serious in the wider community. The Catholic church has little impact on public debate surrounding important questions of marriage, abortion and end of life ethics. It never considers challenges in the world of work, drug addiction and questions surrounding entrepreneurial economic models.

The Catholic church has absolutely nothing to say, nor has it considered questions surrounding robotics, genetic adaptations, the nature of future wars and a value system worth upholding in the twenty-first century. Media commentary has rightly noted, the black hole of ideas, lack of cohesion, drive and energy, and a self-absorbed focus on internal issues of clerical abuse and homosexual clergy.

Australian Catholics are forgetful people who don't know their own history. This impacts on the church in serious ways and inhibits its ability to reflect on who it is and what its future might be. The Australian Catholic church is an organisation that largely does no mission nor actually understands what mission is. The by-product of this lack of mission is its inability to recruit new people and its inability to connect to the wider Australian community. Significantly, because Australian Catholicism knows nothing of its history it has no ability to articulate a future. A people without history is a people without a future. No parish, diocese or Catholic school knows what its history is. Subsequently, the Catholic church is prone to whims, the flavour of the times and jumping on social justice bandwagons as quickly as they come past.

All this because the Catholic church, in its Australian expression, is not bedded down in a solid understanding of what it does, who it is and what it has done well in the past. One of the best examples of this problem was the recent experience of many Bishops and Archbishops. During the 2016 debate and vote on changing the definition of a marriage, to no longer being the exclusive privilege of a man and a woman. Prior to this debate few Catholic leaders made any statements in support of marriage, rarely talked about the importance of marriage in the life of children and failed to discuss the havoc of divorce to both husbands and wives, their children and the wider implications of 50% divorce rates in Australian society. The work to promote marriage and strengthen families was not a priority, particularly cast against issues surrounding, refugees, indigenous culture and a multicultural society.

In August of 2017, some Archbishops circulated short pastoral letters in support of marriage between a man and a woman. They also noted in media outlets that the church's 180,000 employees, mostly teachers, were expected to uphold the church's teaching, "totally" and that defiance would be treated "very seriously". One noted:

> "I would be emphatic that our schools, our parishes exist to teach a Catholic view of marriage, any words or actions which work contrary to that would be viewed very seriously."

As can be imagined, after long years of silence, with no teaching and little discussion about this "Catholic view of marriage", deeply embarrassing situations unfolded for the Archbishops. Many Catholic schools had already been engaging with parents, student bodies and staff, coming to a joint decision that same-sex marriage legislation was a valid viewpoint and firmly within Catholic teaching. Many schools came out in direct opposition to what their Archbishops had said.

The problem with the Archbishops' late engagement with this issue is not difficult to see. If Bishops do not bother to go to their schools, if they do not liaise with staff and parent bodies and if they do not make themselves available to student forums, to teach, argue and contest for the Catholic view, what do they expect will happen?

The days of adherence to church teachings on the word of, distracted Archbishop's are long gone. The Church's teachings are trashed if they are not grappled with and brought into the furnace of public contest. Engagement with Catholic communities and wider Australia is rarely undertaken by the church's leadership, this results in confusion, distress and local chaos.

In the Australian context, the days of assuming Catholic school children, their teachers or regular parishioners know church teaching are past. If we don't contest for and propagate Catholic messages strongly, we can hardly be surprised when Catholics don't understand, and are drawn to popular, secular and easy to understand arguments.

This is the new world in which the church lives, it

is not just an Australian problem. Nevertheless, many Australians are crying out for a church leadership that clearly, with pride and vision is able to instruct and teach the great truths of the church. It is not just a problem of negligent Bishops' but a wider problem where the facts are that the brutal secular culture, we inhabit finds our beliefs of little practical and relevant sense. We speak a language and act in ways the world no longer understands.

This is a book, that is not primarily concerned with what has gone wrong, but with strategies and techniques that will allow the church to thrive, grow and fight for a new and exciting future. In my view there are a number of contending ways forward. One has recently come to life in the context of the American Catholic church: "The Benedict Option". Another has been vigorously tried for over forty years, what I shall refer to as the "Anglican option".

In my estimation both these options are not radically different in that they both end in similar circumstances. I will be suggesting, they are systems with the roots of their failure already growing and visible. A new path I have called "Authentic Mission", it is by far the most difficult, upsetting and seriously uncomfortable, particularly for Western Catholics that have grown lazy, fat and de-energised by the current expression of their faith. It requires fighting and contesting for church values and beliefs in public forum. The future of the Catholic church is not one of comfort, it never has been.

SECTION I

THREATS AND ERRORS

(I) THE BENEDICT OPTION – ROD DREHER

Whether you are an active Catholic or someone who recognises the central role that Christianity plays in forming and sustaining Western values, the fragility of the Australian Catholic Church continues to evoke deep angst and concern. This trend should make us question how Catholicism can be prevented from becoming a shell of its former self.

The most recent foray into this issue is Rod Dreher's "The Benedict Option". This book advocates that Catholics embrace minority status, recognise Catholicism as an "outsider set of values" and live within the secular Western environment. Dreher envisages small Catholic communities in which members live with greater spiritual discipline regarding prayer, worship and commitment to reordering their lives around the faith. Indeed, Dreher goes much further advocating that Catholics turn their homes into a domestic monastery. For Dreher this means maintaining regular times of family prayer and the reading of scripture. Living in a domestic monastery also means putting the life of the church first, even if that means family members do not attend sports programs that schedule games during church worship times. Dreher's model is based strongly on sixth century Benedictine monastic practise which kept outside its walls people and things that were inimical to its purpose. Dreher suggests that a strong correlation is possible when advocating that families strictly limit media, internet and television, both to keep unsuitable content out and to prevent dependence on electronic media.

The narrowing of the Catholic life, that Dreher suggests has many seductive attractions, yet in some serious ways it completely misreads the historical narrative, it misreads the fundamental Catholic call to engagement and transformation of society and it ignores the overwhelming practical failures that such withdrawal decisions have had on the communities of the past.

A case in point is the Viking incursions into France and Anglo-Saxon England in the eighth century. From the 790's small Viking fleets made hit and run attacks along coastal areas. The Viking longships were ideally suited to surprise attacks on poorly defended monasteries and trading centres. The initial response of coastal monasteries was to withdraw to other more isolated locations during summer and return only in winter months, when rough seas made Viking attacks impossible. Yet, throughout the next 120 years, Viking tactics changed, as they began to winter in France and England, returning to Northern homelands less frequently. This resulted in the complete abandonment of all but the most isolated monastic communities.

Whilst some education and learning was maintained

by these isolated monastic communities, the reality of consistent Nordic raids into Western Europe was only stopped by the vigorous resistance of French and Anglo-Saxon Catholic regional kingdoms. The truth of Catholic survival in the eighth century rests with Christian leader such as Alfred the Great and Charles the Bold, both ironically using many converted Nordic soldiers in the defence of their kingdoms.

The Islamic entry into Sicily, Southern Italy and Spain saw no monastic success stories at all, the result for most Catholics at this time was conversion or death. Those that did survive were subjected to the Jizya Tax, restrictions on worship, processions, the use of Church bells and the total loss of administrative control and personal freedom of speech and action. Again, it is only with the rise of Carolingian power in Northern Spain and the later re-conquest of all Spain, that Christians are again able to enter into the fullness of the Christian life.

There is a strong intellectual mythology at play in this alleged harmonising of Christian and Islamic communities, the brutal reality for Spanish Christian communities continues in our own time with the ongoing Egyptian and Turkish control of minority Christian groups in these countries. There is nothing glamorous about Islamic rule for small and isolated Christian communities.

Even with "benevolent" host cultures, the history of small isolated Christian communities is one of failure. In our own time, we are witnessing the erosion of the non-Catholic Amish community, who are under enormous secular pressure and near collapse.

Dreher misreads ancient, medieval and modern Christian history. The church has never sought to form Catholics by nurturing themselves through separation from surrounding society or communities. This was the particular strength of the faith, Catholics can certainly be critical of the world, but their mission was its transformation. There is no history of club or sect behaviour that ever leads anywhere except extinction. Why? Because it goes against the fundamental Christian mission of engaging with individuals and society, resurrecting their lives and values.

The "making of disciples from all nations" (Matthew 28), was not designed to engage a select few but the whole of humanity. This is Christ's fundamental call to his followers.

The crux of Catholicism current problem is not that the secular world has turned against it in overwhelming rejection. The problem is that the secular world no longer knows what Catholicism is. At the core of this new irrelevance is a Catholicism that is unsure of what it stands for, that is beset by its own fears and has lost the confidence to speak with authority. The church has been here before, having for many years sought to avoid clashes with both Nazi's and Communists. The path of appeasement made the years from 1939-1991 long and arduous, yet some individual Catholics always boldly proclaimed Catholic teachings. This is the space we find ourselves in again.

The responsibility of the modern Catholic has not been abrogated because of secular indifference. The Catholic cannot wish for escape or for appeasement through agreement. The work of the church from its foundation has never been given for Catholics alone, it is given for the sake of others. As St Theresa of Avila so powerfully explained, the work of the monastery is not for the monk but for those who undertake the active confrontation with the world.

Henri de Lubac (1896-1991) one of the great theologians of the modern era, never failed to reveal the church's inner mystery to those who are called to faith:

> "fidelity to the grace that makes us members of the Church means that we must take up the demands made upon us, to bring about the salvation of the world, each of us according to our own vocation. And, yet as we labour for this great task, we must also co-operate with God in the individual salvation of those who remain apparently unbelievers" (*Catholicism, Christ and the common testing of man*, page 241).

In less complicated words, yes, we must build the church, but it is not just for us alone and the task of the missionary belongs to us all. Jesus Christ was constantly challenging his followers with a ruthlessly persistent message "Let him who is the greatest among you be as one who serves" (Matthew 23, VII) "Greater love has no man, that he lay down his life for others" (John 15, V13).

Those who belong in the church have a great privilege, but this privilege constitutes a mission to and for others. Perhaps, when Catholics are fearful of the future, or our place in Australian life, we can do no better than to look at the struggle of the Coptic church in Egypt. It has endured fourteen centuries of persecution, yet it has never withdrawn. This church lives profoundly, as Christ notes "to those whom much is given, much is expected" (Luke 12, V48).

(II) JOIN THE CLUB – THE ANGLICAN OPTION

Australian Anglicanism alongside all of the protestant religious groups has largely departed from the Australian religious sphere. They are unfortunately lifeless and wracked with division. It is no longer possible to consider them to be functioning churches, rather they are a small collection of local clubs, numbering on average 30-40 people, focused on internal politics or trendy social issues.

Statistically it is hard to reach any other conclusion, numbers attending some Anglican dioceses are so low they have stopped publishing figures. The major preoccupation of Australia's Anglicans is not the life and teachings of Jesus but a besottedness with tolerance, diversity and justice to the exclusion of all else.

In recent years, the Melbourne Anglican Archdiocese, for example, has concerned itself with a vigorous criticism of Australia's banks, opposing the arrest and detention of David Hicks (an Australian who fought for an overseas Islamic terrorist group), a call for same-sex blessings, a campaign against plastic bags, along with an open policy of refugee entry into Australia. In almost all of these "social justice" issues, the church itself had little skin in the game and offered no financial contributions. The answer in each case was nothing more than a call for increased government spending!

Perhaps, the most fatuous need for media attention came from the Dean of Brisbane Cathedral who announced, a gracious sanctuary to any refugee (within the Cathedral) wishing to escape deportation procedures. The Dean neglected to tell the media that the church operated no programs for refugees, provided no housing and no financial support. Such puerile interventions into serious issues only serves to discredit Christians and the responsible work of Christian charity and service.

The central indicator that this "is club" and not church behaviour, reveals itself when the issues themselves are considered. These "selected issues", constitute the political correctness of the moment. These are controversies derived from the context of the secular media. Their moral authority rests on something called "community values" which is fixed centrally on regulating consumption, providing welfare to all in need and a dramatic redistribution of wealth from the hands of the wealthy, to all those determined to be in need. These values do not take their context from Christian scripture or tradition, but from a socialist view of the world which suggest that societies structures are unjust and need dramatic overhaul. A "church" that seeks to implement such programs is not resting its moral authority on the life of Jesus or on historical Christian tradition but on a secular philosophy found to be wanting in past manifestations.

Such a forlorn moral universe is often portrayed as a great "moral advance", for the modern human and is seen as at last addressing human need. The reality is that such "human need" is really materialism, consumed by a pursuit of welfare and security. In this philosophy only a fool considers human enlightenment to rest in the teachings of Christ, or the call of the church for individual and societal salvation.

The value of Jesus is little more than finding one or two of his teachings that encourage giving to the poor or care of the underdog. In these "club-churches" Christ follows the secular agenda. This agenda can be seen in the new concept of the family that club-churches portray. The family is revealed centrally as the provider of security, no longer is the "extended" family of parents or grandparents living with young families thought to be of value. Financial stability and security for parents and children is the goal above all others. The pursuit of this "security" revolves around both contraception and abortion, both of which are now intimately related to the rights of the family, after all, who would wish to jeopardise "quality of life" with the expense of more than two children. There is no evidence that small family units are either stable or better for children, indeed 50% divorce rate suggests otherwise, yet for the club-church these concerns are simply ignored. Abortion is just a matter of choice and if honestly considered is not sought for medical reasons but because unwanted children are thought to interfere with one's quality of life.

Club-church philosophies have now evolved into active hostility to the "church of the past." In the Christian schools where such a philosophy is rife there is no pride or joy in the beauty of the faith or its extraordinary influence on our society. Students are no longer taught the parables of Christ, the meaning of Christian festivals, the beauty of sacramental life or the remarkable lives of the saints. All the world's religions are included in the curriculum including animist indigenous legends. Students are left to decide their value for themselves. It is undeniable that in such club-churches, students do not attend church themselves and that such churches are largely without any followers under 45 years of age.

All this asks a question and a sub question, can these club-churches survive? And are they a model of relevance the Catholic church might follow? The Anglican club-church and other Protestant groups have been ailing for over 5 decades, they have now reached a critical point of collapse yet will possibly continue in this terminal state for some further decades. Collapsed churches are not new in the world, there is still a Patriarch of Constantinople living in a quiet suburban Istanbul suburb, his former Cathedral is a museum. The Patriarchate of Constantinople is one of the most enduring institutions in the world, yet the patriarch presides over a minuscule number of followers. The Patriarch himself is noted for his environmental work which perhaps suggests this is one of the few areas the Islamic government of

Turkey is prepared to allow him a voice.

The decline of the Anglican church into a club is entirely an act of self-destruction. An over identification and assimilation to a secular culture with few connections into the community, and an ever-desperate desire to find causes to address. All this marks the Anglican church as redundant and unwanted. Be careful where you follow, "can a blind man lead a blind man? Will they both not fall into a pit?" (Luke 6:39).

(II.I) WILL CATHOLICISM TAKE THE ANGLICAN OPTION?

Many Australians are prone to taking short cuts, it's a tendency we all have, and some maintain all their lives. Yet, persistence, dedication, hard work and failure are central to future success (failure is central to the outcome for without failure no real learning occurs). This is not a message we like to hear, yet it is the only message of success. The world is littered with people who think they are talented yet have achieved nothing with their lives. Winston Churchill was fond of saying "There is no such thing as genius, just sheer bloody hard work" Abraham Lincoln went in a slightly different direction "Show me the man who has succeeded, and I will ask only of his failures". Many Catholics have a strong desire to follow the Anglican path as a strategy for relevance, justice and future successes. Copying the Anglican model of assimilation to the world is a short-cut Catholicism would be ill-advised to take.

At various points of its history, the Vatican has been known to advocate for allegedly short-term solutions in efforts to relieve oppression or persecution. In the 1960's Popes John XXIII and Paul V initiated a new policy called Ostpolitik. This policy sought to find a "modus non moriendi" – a way of not dying for churches caught behind the iron curtain in communist controlled countries. The policy included an end to public criticism of communist regimes and a negotiating process intended to give Catholics some minimal freedom within communist structure. The results were a disaster, with Vatican weakness leading to greater persecution. The long-term imprisonment of many priests and laity and the complete infiltration of the Hungarian, East German and Czechoslovakian Catholic church by communist spy agencies.

This Vatican "engagement" with the communist system disempowered Catholic human right advocates, silenced the faithful in their efforts at local evangelism but most seriously, weakened the worldwide Catholic church in its wider responsibility to stand up for their faith. When a faithfully rich and colourful Catholic church seeks benefits from colourless and lifeless regimes, a bland and lifeless Catholicism is all that can emerge, such is the result of worldly compromise.

The modern church continues to be at risk of lifeless compromise in our own day. The recognition of communist China as a valid partner for the Vatican, in the full knowledge that freedom of expression, free Catholic life is again compromised. An insipid and vanilla expression of the faith is not what Christ gave up his life to bring about.

Challenges to the Catholic faith also exist in Modern Europe. In September of 2019, the German episcopate adopted a framework for its upcoming synod assembly which seeks to review church teaching on sexual morality, the role of women in ministry, priestly life and discipline and the separation of power in the church. The concept of local Catholic jurisdictions re-fining doctrine and changing Catholic practices to be acceptable to local culture is indistinguishable from the practices of the club-church. The Australian Plenary Conference set for 2020 seems keen to copy this Agenda. The Catholic church is a church that has one faith, one sacramental system and one discipline, it cannot be a club!

This is the foundation of Catholic mission; the message and salvation of Christ is the same in every time and every place. Certainly, the talents and vocations of local Catholics are recognised as unique and add dimensions and layers to Catholic truths, yet they cannot be a replacement for Catholic divine revelation. These challenges to Catholicism have always existed and will continue to exist into the future. The importance of Catholic clarity regarding its role and mission cannot be understated, particularly in our day.

(III) THE PROGRAMMED CHURCH: THE ERROR OF ALPHA AND DIVINE RENOVATION

The hard truth for most Catholic Parishes is that we do no mission. Mission is not running an additional mass or a bible study, nor a prayer group in the home of a parishioner. These actions may have a missional dimension, particularly if they are able to attract some newcomers but at a foundational level, they are not themselves about mission.

Mission is not primarily about lapsed Catholics, the "lost" children of Catholics, or those who self-nominate as Catholics and then proceed to ignore mass and most teachings of the church. There is nothing "Catholic" in these individuals with their views on their heritage or their family history as "Catholic" or their warm feelings about their grandparents who seemed such good and idealised faithful Catholics, your family history, heritage or childhood memories does not make you a Catholic.

Mission at the most basic is an action of choosing to "live" and "to be" the faith, with all of the cost that entails, it is a concrete decision for Christ. In sporting terms, it means, paying your membership and attending the games. If you do not do these things for your football team, in what way exactly are you a supporter?

I am sure that people with fond memories of a "Catholic childhood" or "Catholic grandparents" are well intentioned and that these are vital personal memories. Nevertheless, they are not vital support for the church. These "Catholic affections" are indistinguishable from those who know nothing about the faith and have never cared about Catholicism. The starting place is the same. This is the fundamental concern of the church, "make Catholics" – create individuals who buy memberships, go to the games and live the team in their heart and soul.

This is what mission is about "go and make disciples" – your family history is of no consequence, your current yes or no to the church is! In truth, your Catholicism comes down to what you do, not what you hope you might do, or are thinking about. The Catholic faith is to be lived, wrestled with and fought for.

So, we can see that mission is a hard-starting place, a long journey, and one that is full of many disappointments, dead ends and blatant failures. It was ever thus, or Christ himself would not have told us about wolves in sheep's clothing, about persecution, family rejection and sometimes crucifixion. It's easy to say the church needs mission, easy to see the things the church does badly, easy to suggest we are dying of 1,000 cuts, but the question of mission is always the same, what will you do? What CPR will you give, how will you bandage the church.

So before anything, mission is a "fighting attitude", a "spirit of doing", a desire to live the faith, wrestle with God, shape and change the world, fail and yet start again, Mission is not glamour, churches full of thousands, lovely choirs and celebrity speakers, it is shear bloody hard work, that will cost. No wonder "the harvest is plentiful, but the labourers are few" (Matt 9:37).

When it comes to mission, Catholics are prone to making a great mistake. Many Catholics look at the large Evangelical churches, see the apparent youth of the gatherings, the large numbers, the vibrant and attractive music and the strong emotional attachment, that this form of Christianity seems to evoke.

The obvious question, is why can't we do that? What's wrong with Catholicism that so many young families find it boring and monotonous? Why do we appear to have so little growth and why have we embarked on policies of merging and closing parish centres? All of these are good questions, but they have elicited an intrinsically mistaken approach.

In observing these new evangelist churches, we have sought to copy their models which are profoundly uncatholic and in complete candour have not created long-term Christians.

And so, we have witnessed Catholic parishes turn themselves into program churches, with two of the most common being Alpha and Divine Renovation. Both of these programs are at bottom, copies of the

Evangelical churches and the theology that underpins them.

This theology has as a central core the development of the individual and the centrality of making a personal commitment to the person of Jesus. This theological stance is all powerful in evangelical thinking and needs to be constantly renewed, reaffirmed and enhanced. Catholics also agree that this theology is important but our theological stance is developed within the mystical body of Christ, it is unfolded in a deep understanding of the trinity, of the calling to enter the divine life through the eucharistic sacrifice, of devotion to Mary as the mother of both the church and us and of transforming our faith away from ourselves to being a vehicle that changes the world.

The programmed church knows little of these deep strands of Catholicism, its central work is concentrated on a positive experience of worship, of liturgy that encourages feeling good, of creating a vibe, encouraging a friendly atmosphere, of "upbeat music" and of creating enthusiasm and expectation of an experience of Christ for the individual participant in the worship.

Naturally, there is no reason why a mass should not have aspects of this liturgical experience but significant problems arise when the central experience of mass is constantly a focus on the emotions, when the liturgy must continually provide new speakers, new themes, new discussion topics, new forms of praise, punchy sermons, personal stories of success and strong examples of Christ in the life of the individual. Fundamentally, Catholic liturgy is not just for the edification of the individual but for the development of the body of Christ, so that we might transform the world – this is why we are brought together in Christ – for the transformation of the world. Any church that does not concentrate on that dimension of Christian life is not truly Christian and runs the risk of a hollow form of Christian expression.

The high turnover of evangelical congregations suggest difficulty in developing and maintaining the faith. A church that provides only enthusiasm, good vibes and emotional connectiveness for participants is good as far as it goes, but it does not go very far.

If I sound perplexed and disappointed with Catholics that wish to copy evangelicals, I am sorry, I do not wish to undermine anyone's desire to make Catholicism more relevant to modern Australians, yet we have a far deeper and greater offering to the world, we must be bold enough to trust our history, culture, values in the person of Jesus in highlighting and showing the world the fullness of who we are.

Rather than "program" churches there are a number of central underlying Catholic planks on which our local parishes must be based, the expressions may be very different, but the beams, supports and foundational slab are always the same for an authentic Catholic parish life.

Primarily, we are not a people that is affected by the changing race, sex and gender politics. We are not to be seduced by worldly fears, be they of economic collapse, climate disasters or our own place in the world – our role is societal transformation, this must always remain our essential position, for Christ has charged us with transforming the world.

We are not called to adapt to the world but to be its trigger for transformation. This is the reason in the midst of great change, the church upholds the value of marriage, of commitment to one person, of love of family and children, of the dignity of work and the support of the lost. These are not "attractive" values in modern Australia, yet in a confused and depressed world they are fundamental to the light that Christ offers the world. Perhaps, we will be the last Australians to think of relationships in such terms, yet this only ensures the world will need us more in the near future.

The church is also the mainspring and driving force in a number of key institutions and attitudes that we must always affirm and need to do so again in modern Australia. Catholicism has created and highlighted the centrality of freedom, democracy and the rule of law. Our recent Australian expression of these "Catholic values" is under significant attack, but we in our parish life have been too silent and lacked vigour in our support of those who still uphold them. The voice of the Catholic church needs to be heard by those who seek to challenge totalitarian, dictatorship, sham democracies or those who erode freedom in our universities, our workplaces, our political environments. When political correctness costs people their livelihoods, hurts their families or damages their communities, there the church must speak. Parish life is also founded on such values. How a parish seeks to defend and inspire such values, are all local initiatives, and can differ widely, yet they must be affirmed again.

Being local is one of the important aspects of Catholic parish life that has been undermined in recent years, mostly through centrality. When diocese encourage giving for centralised causes, I am not suggesting this is not valuable or important work. Yet it does have the effects of directing local resources away from the parish and usually ensures that a "connection" with the centralised cause cannot easily be generated in the local area.

Perhaps the most serious consequence of allowing funding for good works to be managed centrally is that parishes have stopped "owning" and "operating" their own local initiatives. Without these local initiatives, run by local parish people, the community in which a parish resides, doesn't see or know of Catholic good works. It is not long before the wider community thinks that Catholics do little for their local area. A diocese in trouble is one that only points to its hospitals and schools (most of which are government funded) as examples of its community interaction. The face of the church must be local, and local parishioners must be responsible for that work. Until we are driven to do mission locally, we will remain a disconnected organisation that sits on the corner, but one whom most people continue to drive past.

A concerning by-product of not acting locally has been an erosion of both Catholic culture and Catholic spirituality. The role of Our Lady as a driving force for Catholic initiatives and spiritual development is visibly diminished in many local parishes.

Progressive priests have removed statues of Our Lady, devotional places, even the lighting of candles for a loved one, or a personal concern, has disappeared from our parishes and are non-existent in our schools.

Catholic parishes who won't highlight our lady's example along with the example of the saints may well be progressive and concerned with progressive issues, but they are not churches that Australians are joining. The number of modern Australians who know nothing of the saints, the martyrs, the example and history of local "heroes" or even the reasons their parish was formed, primarily hurt their own Catholicism. "One Holy Catholic and Apostolic" is a wonderful phrase from our creed, but it is based on real people, who struggled. thrived and lived their faith. Without their stories we are not standing on the shoulder of giants but the quagmire of progressive cultured fads and passing fashions.

In our history these swinging trends have never helped the church to survive and grow. The roots of Catholic culture cannot be bedded in climate change, indigenous dreamtime, transgender issues or whatever will come next, but is the example of resilience given to us by saints, such as Max Kolbe, Thomas More, John Fisher, Therese of Lisieux and John Paul II.

Their lives and examples were always local, but their Catholic and cultural embodiment proved to be universal. We again need to highlight and contest for their legacy. They are the future of the church. We all need heroes as examples. There is nothing sadder than young Catholics who know nothing of the saints but fear for their future without examples of God's benevolence and support for the world's future.

In many parishes, Catholic action and deeds have ceased. Yet, we are called to be primarily people of action and energy. For this reason, it is crucial that local Catholic parishes support locals in need, whether that be single mums, families struggling to survive economically, young people disengaged or those involved with drugs or alcohol. Supporting the local community in this way is an indispensable first step in developing and achieving mission as it gives parishes an important sense of self, an example of Catholic culture and faith in action. If your local community cannot clearly see and identify what you are on about, then in what way are you portraying your Catholicity to those around you? Yes, culture and faith should be number one, in who we are and what you do, but it must be local and it must be "deeds" based.

There is always a great deal of hidden suffering

and despair in every community, our nurture of those in anguish or hardship has always been a measure of what the church is about.

From its inception the church has been deeply involved with those who suffer, because it is part of Christs mission to change the world, confront evil and to heal people over the "long-haul". There are many imposters in this field, yet the church has always been successful in difficult circumstances because it brings community to bear on damaged individuals. It does not bring fly by night evangelists with alleged healing gifts. The Catholic notion of healing is community based and rests on the manifold gifts of the whole community. In this way healing becomes a deep and two-way process. This is another example of Catholic culture in action.

Catholic parishes are fundamentally curative in temperament, yet we have stopped this attribute of our work. Developing healing ministries should be a dimension of every parish. I do not advocate for what this might look like and what the particular form may take but this is another essential local ministry that needs to be rediscovered.

These are all ways in which the Catholic culture of the parish are put into workable and practical outcomes. If we do no healing then we forsake a central tenant of Christ's teaching and heritage to us.

> "As you go, preach this message, The kingdom of God is near, heal the sick, raise the dead,

cleanse the lepers, drive out demons, freely you have received, freely give," (Matthew 10:8) or do we no longer believe that these things are possible?

At the base of all these Catholic cultural dimensions is the inspiration of the Holy Spirit, which for Catholicism has always been a spirit of freedom. A sovereignty and privilege to serve the Lord, serve our communities and change the world, we cannot be afraid to claim our freedom, whether that be freedom of speech, freedom to preach, freedom to uphold sacramental life (particularly the sanctity of confession) to build churches where we wish, to speak out against injustice or indifference. The church was not created by Christ to be silent or indifferent to the world's anguish nor to be afraid of communists, dictators, other religions or politically correct democracies. As Christ himself has noted "I have told you these things so that in me you may have peace. In the world you will have tribulation. But take courage, I have overcome the world (John 16:33).

When we claim our freedom and act boldly, we are truly Catholic.

(IV) THE THERAPEUTIC CHURCH

The Therapeutic Church can be found in most cities of the Western world. In the Australian context they are usually distinctly marked by large billboards at the front of their churches spotlighting a particular human weakness or wish. "Are you lonely? Are you depressed? Are you looking for a partner or a community? Do you wish for a new you? ...then we are the church for you!"

Many of these churches target specific groups of people. In inner cities areas it is often overseas university students who naturally are without friendship groups, and might be struggling in a new cultural environment or whose language proficiency may be weak. The desire for friends and community connections are strong in each one of us. But the veracity of these billboards is that they are not designed to primarily fix human problems but to increase Church membership.

A powerful sub message will usually involve an appeal to Jesus, all these desires for healing and fulfilment of life's dreams and hopes comes through the person of Jesus. Giving your life to Jesus or allowing Jesus to "save" you will play a central role in the healing process. Jesus will bless you; Jesus will develop your life; Jesus will make you a better person. In broad terms Catholics will be of a similar mind yet a narrow Christology that portrays Jesus as singularly focused on the healing or fulfilment of the individual in a serious misreading of the life and mission of Christ.

In Catholic theology salvation is overwhelming found in service, service to the body of Christ and service through the body of Christ. Catholicism is not an individualised expression or dimension of life. Indeed, calling and vocation have little to do with the individual but are a response to the call of God and often they are against the wishes of the individual themselves. In Catholicism individuals can definitely come to the fullness of life, happiness and a sense of purpose, but that is always through the body of Christ and acting in the name of Christ whose primary call is to make disciples of all nations so that the world may be changed. Individual happiness or fulfilment may not obviously enter the equation.

The martyrdom that some Christians experience suggests that fulfillment and happiness are not Christ's greatest gifts to his followers. Hardship, difficulty and burdens will also be part of the Christian life, for ultimately it is not a life centred on individual conversion but on community service.

The experience of many of these "therapeutic churches" is one of high membership turnover and sometimes an experience of Jesus that didn't seem to work in the long run. If Christ is only for our fulfilment or to fix our problems, it is not surprising that Jesus would challenge these "one dimensional" views of himself. Early in the Gospel narrative, Jesus calls disciples to follow him, it is important to note that in all these calls to vocation, Christ laid out two fundamental dimensions "Repent, for the Kingdom of Heaven is at hand and follow me and I will make you fishes of men" (Matthew 4, 14-20). The vocation of following Jesus is one of "changing" your own life and then adding others to the body of Christ. Jesus does not promise personal fulfillment, happiness or a wonderful life. Indeed, for Jesus these may be seen as distractions from the primary task of constructing the Kingdom of God.

The cost of following Jesus and acting to draw others to Christ may well be extreme. Jesus constantly talks about this cost; it is the primary reason people draw back from Jesus and a foundational underlay for many of Christ's parables regarding all the things that choke or disrupt the calling of God. The truth of vocation is that it is not always pleasant, easy or fulfilling to those who undertake its path.

In contrast therapeutic churches concentrate on you and your dreams, what are your hopes, wishes and plans for the future? Christianity then becomes a method or a vehicle for your fulfillment and Christ becomes the way to achieve your goals.

In essence this is fundamentally anti-Catholic and a serious distortion of the life of faith and the formation of Christ's body. There is no doubt that aspects of life can be discouraging and that some individuals can be crushed or blocked in life and stop functioning. Catholic parishes have no wish to see this happen and the Catholic Church also has a significant healing ministry orientating individuals towards a fuller and more complete life, yet this is not new life, where you take up a pedestal with yourself at the centre but a life which enables you to restart or undertake your vocation. It is vocation that is at both the centre of the individual Catholic life and at the centre of Catholic mission. We are not answering our calling but Christs!

There is also a debilitating notion that many therapeutic churches promote strongly. That is that God blesses you and wants you to succeed in your life's dreams. I know of no individual life where this is true. If success is financial security, a happy family, motivated children and a wide circle of loving and respectful friends, even this is the narrowest possible definition of success.

It is not the promise of Christ in scripture, in the life of his disciples or the life of Christ crucified himself. All lives are a mixture of success, failure, re-evaluation in our lives, knowing that we can rarely undertake a task without constantly checking in with God. The nature of humanity is one of partial completion, restarting and hoping to do better in the future. The role of humanity is to start the journey of mission in hope, it is God's business to bring it to fulfillment, in his own particular way and timing.

Churches that talk of success in your life, of your "wishing to succeed" or even of the price you must pay for success – even if that be a restoration of health, are fundamentally "selling" a distorted version of the faith.

Authentic Mission and authentic Christian life are not primarily about us, uppermost is the life of Christ lived out to the best of our ability. As St Paul notes "it is no longer I who live but Christ who lives in me" (Galatians 2.20), yes, we want individuals to be healthy, fulfilled and joyous but foremost we are followers of Christ, residing in his call to us.

In this way we are partnered with Christ and bring about his Kingdom. The Catholic life is above all, a life of vocation, that remains our central purpose and task.

(V) THE SOCIAL JUSTICE CHURCH

The significant emphasis on social justice in the Catholic Church and most other Australian Churches is a key symbol of the irrelevance of the church to the life and concerns of the majority of Australians.

Nevertheless, Churches and Bishops continue to push the relevance of social justice to a fair, just and moral society as an indicator that these Churches are still fit to speak to wider Australia.

Wider Australia has not been concerned with the statements and agendas of Church agencies for many decades. This is a harsh fact, yet these Churches are living in a delusional frame of mind.

They are ignored by governments, state and federal, universities, think-tanks and peak bodies. Indeed, the condition of these agencies is ailing and unhealthy to the point that they are unable to mount or sustain campaigns on ideas or projects that directly affect them. They are only capable of parroting the left-wing views of others. The thoughts and considerations of the Catholic Bishops conference has not evoked press or community discussions for decades. A Ho-Hum, who cares attitude pervades Australian life in relation to Church welfare agencies.

This can be observed in the three continual concerns that the Church has pushed over the last 20 years. These are indigenous issues, refugees and increased welfare payments. These are the only issues the Australian press is likely to publish and Churches bring nothing new to these social justice concerns. At best they add a heart-warming reassurance to secular concerns. The agenda must be correct even the Churches recognise its importance, at base the Churches remain irrelevant, fringe dwellers to these issues and do not bring a unique Catholic or transformational attitude to any of these questions. Churches that continue to promote and push these agendas are talking to themselves, perhaps they still provide comfort for the adherents of these Churches, but they have zero impact on Australian society.

In recent decades, Churches with a prominent social justice agenda have witnessed the spread and enlargement of aid agency bureaucracy. This bureaucracy has significantly dissipated away from the provision of an actual welfare service into one that aggressively undertakes advocacy, including lobbying national and state agencies engaging in promotion of particular agencies seeking to change government and other authority viewpoints. Serious questions are arising as to who these agencies actually represent, for whom do they speak and can it be accurately concluded that they represent the Church?

Increasingly, these bodies have developed a stand-alone life of their own, often representing the political agendas of the people who work within them. Most of these organisations are charitable entities, are filled with unelected boards and directors and are primarily concerned with the aims and objectives of their charitable founder or order, all this is well and good but in what way are they accurately speaking and advocating for their churches? In many cases there needs to be stronger statements that these aid agencies are private organisations and not connected to the life of the Church in meaningful ways.

Perhaps, a more serious outcome of the growth of these agencies is the emaciation that they have had on local parish welfare and mission. Their connection to a local parish is usually little more than a dedicated Sunday collection, once a year. Most parishes have never seen a representative of these organisations, they do not operate locally, so their connectedness with the wider Church amounts to small change placed in an annual appeal envelope. Again, in what way do these agencies know anything of the life of a local parish or what the local needs might be? Sadly, the pervasion of these organisations often leads to an atrophy at the parish level and a parish illusion that we are doing our bit, although the benefits of such collections are rarely seen at the local parish level.

It is my viewpoint that these twin developments within the Church, the significant growth of centralised aid agencies and the emaciation of parish welfare initiatives, has caused the Church to overlook and become substantially disconnected from the critical issue that is facing Australia today.

This imperative and crucial issue is employment.

The health of a nation rests on the provision of meaningful long-term employment. The future hope of the individual and nation rests on employment, the moral security of a nation rests on employment, for this is the key way society illustrates to its citizens and future generations that they are valued and respected, that they will share in the collective wealth and benefits of the society.

Without a focus on work no society can truly speak of morality, values or care of its citizens. When work is missing, the loyalty of individuals will flounder and centrally the values that Churches alleged to hold precious such as marriage, family, involvement in Church and wider community will crumble.

This is currently happening in modern Australia and the Australian Churches are oblivious to these changing realities. The impact of the emphasis on social justice that many Churches display has been a disaster for the Church. It has resulted in a disconnection between parish and diocese, yet more abysmal is the resultant powerlessness and languid effect on local parishes. Parishes are now unable to do local mission, no longer have the skills to undertake welfare initiatives and subsequently find that they cannot attract or hold new people into their communities. Mission and welfare and healthy parishes are inextricably linked. But they must be local, run by locals and benefit local residents. As most Australian Churches no longer do this, we suffer ineffectiveness and irrelevance.

As it currently stands, the provisions of social justice initiatives by Church agencies also has a horrible effect on recipient individuals. Are we any longer changing lives? Are we actually benefitting struggling families? Do we make any impact on the welfare of our younger Australians? The statistical analysis of these issues just continues to get worse, indeed we are not causing Australian adults to act like adults, we are in fact holding people in dependency. And, in the middle of these welfare programs is there any Christian dimensions that might challenge or change a life? In truth Church mission agencies just mirror the agendas of secular agencies. Do we ask for any responsiveness to those who receive or participate in welfare programs – no we don't, because we no longer have the local knowledge that builds relationships and points the way through example and challenge. If we do not ask a welfare recipient for some time, effort or help in return just how do we really provide the benefit and change that comes through dignity?

In many ways Churches that rely on social justice agencies have misread the life and teachings of Jesus. These agencies have buzzwords like peace and inclusion, yet Jesus does not promote these things as values above all, for Christ the formula was actually about challenge and change with a strong acknowledgement that these would cost!

Finally, young Australians have largely left the Church, this is a fact. Young Australians have abandoned the Church because they think it has nothing of value to offer them or their future society. Perhaps they are right, to a generation riddled with anxiety and depression we need a message of challenge and transformation. Its time our welfare and our mission reflected this.

(VI) CLIMATE, CAPITALISM AND LOST SHEPHERDS

As Australians enters into its 2020 plenary council, it is worth considering some of the concerns facing Australian Catholicism into the near future. Without doubt, the pontificate of Francis has sought to align the Catholic church within the global climate change movement. In addition, unfortunately, Pope Francis has radically supplemented Vatican thinking on climate change with some fallacious ethical considerations of financial markets, trade relationships and wealth creation.

The Holy Father promulgated his encyclical "Laudato si, mi signori" (Praise to you, my Lord) in 2015, covering issues of climate change, environmental protection and sustainable development. The world's attention was drawn to the document for its use of an austere and grim form of language which the world's media constantly highlighted in its most oft quote phrase:

> "The earth is beginning to look more and more like an immense pile of filth."

The encyclical further notes that current energy policies are based on the "false notion" that an "infinite quantity of energy and resources are available." And that the world must implement new energy and economic systems to ensure "intergenerational solidarity" by protecting the needs of future generations.

Whilst such statements display a noble concern for the future of our planet and our children, it also raises the genuine question of how accurate, is the Pope's understanding of both history and the worlds recent use of natural resources?

If we reflect on human history, in any period of time prior to the industrial revolution of the 1800's we can confidently label the overwhelming experience of humans to be "lonely poor, nasty, brutal and short" (Thomas Hobbes 1651 AD).

For most humans, life was filled with malnutrition and starvation, filthy water, a myriad of disease, the absence of any sanitary practice and constant war. The suggestion that our planet was previously a benevolent natural world, of consistent climate and idyllic pastoral life is not born out by facts.

Such a world never existed for the vast majority of humans. Of all historical institutions the Catholic church knows such a view to have not been the truth. To propagate such a view positions the encyclical on fundamentally deceitful foundations.

Regrettably, Pope Francis continues this deception in his analysis of the post-1800 AD human experience. He asserts in section 44:

> "We are conscious of the unruly growth of many cities which have become unhealthy to

live in, not only because of pollution but as a result of urban chaos, poor transportation, visual pollution and noise."

In section 46, he suggests:

"Global change includes the effects of technological innovations on employment, social exclusion, an inequitable distribution and consumption of energy, social breakdown, increased violence and new forms of social aggression, drug trafficking, growing drug use by young people and loss of identity."

Lamentably, the Francis encyclical fails to consider the true advancement and progression of humanity over the last 200 years. He ignores the colossal advances in medical science, the complete erasure of malaria, cholera, tuberculosis and polio. He disregards the discovery of anti-biotics, vaccinations, along with anaesthesia and surgical techniques, the necessary prerequisite for advanced and lifesaving surgery and the basis of the huge increase in human life span.

During this period, the internal combustion engine replaces oxen and horses and improved seeds and irrigation uphold crop harvest levels that sustain millions. The invention of electricity transforms our buildings and public spaces making them safe and greatly increasing transport and travel options. The average Westerner has increased their life expectancy from as little as 46 years in 1900 to over 80 years today.

In China 99% of its population now has electricity up from 8% in 1945, Chinese life expectancy is also around 80 years adding an additional 32 years since 1960 and a citizenship 90% wealthier than that year.

These improvements are indeed miraculous, yet they are based on a proven formula, a free enterprise system, improved legal protections and property rights for "ordinary people", but above all cheap energy including coal, oil, natural gas, hydro electrical systems and nuclear energy. This power sustains factories, schools, farms, hospitals, homes, offices, refrigerators, air conditioners, computers, televisions and life sustaining medical treatment.

For the encyclical to suggest that the modern world is a technique for possession and dominance and that our current financial system is focused solely on economic gain and incapable of considering human dignity is completely unproven by the plainly visible improvements to human life for the majority of humanity on our planet.

This encyclical is a misrepresentation of the current state of the world. In 1815 one billion people inhabited our planet. Today it is seven billion. Unquestionably, there is still much to do. In India more than 300 million people still lack electricity, in sub-Saharan Africa 730 million still cook with wood or animal dung. On average 5 million of these people die each year from lung disease or unclean water. Breathing smoke from open fires and lack of refrigeration, which increases intestinal disease are still number one killers of humans throughout the world.

The encyclical of Pope Francis counsel's restrictions on fossil fuels and advocates for renewal energy mandates. Such a position would reduce living standards in poorer nations, perpetrate squalor and ensure that reliable and affordable energy which develops and improves jobs, health, food, living standards and the environment, be denied to those most in need. This cannot be an ethical position for the Catholic church, nor one adopted in plenary by Australian Catholics.

(VII) VATICAN SILENCE IN CHINA

Xi Jing Ping is the Chairman of everything in Communist China. He is the Head of the Communist party, the President, the Chief of the Military, all power flows into his direct control. Civil, military and strategic oversight belongs exclusively to him and to the Communist party of China. There is no other power or leadership sources in China, no independent judiciary, no regional or community leadership activists, no alterative educational, religious or social groupings. Power is invested in one political party only and in one individual, as the head of this party.

On March 2018, President Xi was voted "leader for life" of the Chinese Communist Party. Effective opposition to the rule of Xi is currently non-existent. There is no free press, no free internet, no uncontrolled communication or telephone networks, there is no free religious expression and no freedom of association nor the ability for individuals or groups to organise or transmit information that may be considered harmful to Chinese Communism. Foreign companies who conduct business in China are heavily monitored, their communications observed, and their movements and contacts followed and documented. A vast network of surveillance camera's constantly monitors the movements of citizens, commonly portrayed as security to detect crime and terrorists.

The truth is that facial recognition cameras monitor and collect information on your friends, travels, web searches, even shopping habits ensuring that communist officials know more about their citizens than any other nation on earth.

Andrew Hastie is the member for Canning (WA) in the Australian Parliament, a former special air service regiment soldier who has served in Afghanistan and most recently Chair of the Parliamentary Joint Committee on Intelligence and Security. Hastie has noted strongly, how authoritarian the Chinese state has increasingly become and claimed that China's actions in the world challenge Australia with its greatest democratic, economic and security test in coming decades. Hastie makes a powerful and valid statement on Australian vulnerability:

> "right now, our greatest vulnerability lies not in our infrastructure but in our thinking, that intellectual failure makes us institutionally weak. If we don't understand the challenges ahead for our civil society, in our parliaments, in our universities, in our private enterprises, in our charities then choices will be made for us. Our sovereignty, our freedom, will be diminished".

It is very important for the Catholic Church worldwide and for Australian Catholics to also be alerted to the serious threat that China poses to fundamental freedoms.

In Australia, Catholics take many freedoms for granted particularly the freedom to express the teachings of Christ to a wider world, increasingly in China, this freedom is overridden, restricted or violently crushed. Catholics have been on the receiving end of decades of persecution, arrest, detention and discrimination.

The Chinese Communist party has no incentive to grant basic rights of freedom of faith to Catholics, indeed years of repressive behaviour towards Catholics, continues into current times with no signs of changing Communist practices.

Recently, we have witnessed the repression on the basic freedoms of Hong Kong citizens. Chinese communists are more authoritarian, and less concerned with the rights of Chinese citizens than at any stage in their 70-year history.

The Chinese military is also undertaking an aggressive regional build up which despite many warm words of peaceful intentions have seriously worried regional states including Japan, South Korea, Vietnam, the Philippines, Singapore and Australia. Freedom of navigation through the South China sea is largely prohibited with few regional countries wishing to engage the "peaceful" actions of the Chinese state.

The reality for those who live near China, particularly the people of Hong Kong and Taiwan is that economic power is quickly transforming into geo-political power, with the Chinese state seeking to influence, control and ensure that near neighbours, trading partners and its own citizens are conforming to the day-to-day dictates of the Chinese Communist party.

Chinese military ambitions are also expanding. China now operates a military base in the strategically important Gulf of Aden nation of Djibouti, giving it significant access to the Indian Ocean and blue water naval capabilities beyond its immediate region. Its militarisation of the critical trade routes within the South China sea is now complete, allowing China to impose military pressure and inhibit all but the strongest nations from using the region as a through traffic trade route.

Perhaps, the most concerning of all issues in China's global rise is its brutal repression of internal dissent. This repression is especially significant towards ethic and religious minorities and those who seek to highlight lack of democratic freedom or freedom of speech. The disturbances that have recently flared in Hong Kong point to the increasing desire of Chinese communists to control and restrict citizens, political movements and prohibit calls of democratic freedom from evolving.

All this begs a deeper question for Catholics, what is the Vatican doing in relation to this increased surveillance, control and repression of Chinese citizens, especially Catholics? Why hasn't the Vatican expressed any concern or focused media attention on the severe clampdowns of personal and religious freedoms? Why has the Pope not spoken about the disturbances in Hong Kong and their wider ramifications? Why is his Holiness not defending free speech, democratic rights or indeed the rights of practising Catholics within China?

These are serious questions and the Vatican's silence in relation to these essential human concerns, not only brings ignominy on Pope Francis and the wider church but more importantly allows repression and human rights violation to continue without scrutiny. When the Vatican is silent on such issues it betrays the fundamental call of Christ to set individuals and peoples free. When the church refuses to speak on such issues it betrays its mission but more centrally risks damaging the very notion of who it is.

What has caused the Vatican to be so frail and disempowered in its responses to severe Chinese attacks upon human rights and to be acquiescent to the persecution of its own Catholic faithful?

Late in 2018 The Vatican authorised a largely secret agreement with the Chinese Communist party which advised Chinese Catholic Priests and Bishops to comply with Chinese law and register officially with the government. This process has additionally seen recognition of former "State authorised Catholic Churches" as now being in communion with the Pope (a fundamental definition of what it means to be a Catholic).

The consequences for the Vatican have already been both disappointing and grave. Many Bishops and Priests recognised by the Vatican have continued to adhere to membership if the Chinese Communist party. A dual loyalty which seriously questions their commitment to the worldwide Catholic Church. Hong Kong's emeritus Cardinal Joseph Zen has rightly warned such an ongoing situation could "risk the death of the Catholic faith in China."

A Vatican statement of June 2019 acknowledges the quagmire, that the agreement, rushed and naively advocated by Pope Francis is not working. The statement acknowledges "the limitations and intimidatory pressures faced by many Catholics."

Cardinal Zen has sadly noted:

> "The Chinese Communist party has already reneged on its promises to respect Catholic doctrine."

The Cardinal further suggests that many:

> "...underground Priests and those who have worked with great tenacity to achieve changes had hoped for the support of the Holy See".

It would appear such hopes have been thoroughly misplaced. The decision of Pope Francis to "trust and engage" with Chinese Communists is already a decision with severe consequences for Chinese Catholics on the ground. Chinese Communists are unable to tolerate opposition, know nothing of democratic process and have shown brutal ruthlessness against Tibetans, Uyghurs, Falun Gong and now appear focused on Hong Kong and Catholicism.

We in Australia can privately laugh at the Qantas Kowtow to Chinese communists which sees Qantas no longer refer to Taiwan as the Republic of China. The Papal Kowtow will never be seen in writing but is witnessed clearly in Vatican silence on freedom and democratic hope in Hong Kong.

(VIII) THE NEW SOCIALISM

The Catholic Church has grappled and contested with Communion and Socialism throughout most of the twentieth century and into the twenty-first. The suffering experienced by Catholics and other Christians during this time has been profound. It is often not known that most of our martyrs have been produced in the twentieth century, the vast majority of these are individuals and communities resisting and keeping the faith alive in the face of Communist and socialist persecution. This situation continues to remain and is borne by our Catholic brothers and sisters into our current years. China, North Korea, Cuba, Venezuela, Vietnam, Sudan and Uzbekistan are just a few nations that still persecute the faith into the current day.

Nevertheless, despite this great suffering and the vigorous attempts to destroy Catholicism, it is only in a few places and driven by determined individuals, has the Church successfully resisted and contended with these malevolent systems. Sadly, the church in most instances chooses the road of accommodation and little resistance. The failures of the church in Cuba, Russia, Hungary, East Germany and most of the Eastern European states, sees the Catholic church remaining in suspicion from their host communities, who remember their complicity and fearful accommodation.

Our historical low point was the policy of

"Ostpolitik" which was initiated in the Vatican of the 1960's under the papacy of John XXIII and Paul VI. The policy was shaped by the strategic goal of developing a "modus non moriendi". A way of not dying which centred on the Vatican no longer publicly criticising socialist regimes. The results were calamitous, witnessing a vicious spying penetration of the church hierarchy in Hungary, Russia, East Germany and Cuba and the mass arrest of many Catholic lay people striving for a better life, which included basic freedoms.

The Catholic church has not yet recovered in these nations. It is really only with the election of Cardinal Karol Wojtyla to the papacy in 1978 that effective resistance to socialist assaults on the church could be commenced. It is important to note that Pope John Paul II didn't overly emphasise political or economic messages but cultural and spiritual ones. It was the emphasis on God given human dignity that challenges a socialist culture centred exclusively on selfish economic rights and on alleged competition with an "evil capitalist class" which existed mythically in Western nations.

Tragically in 21st century Australia, a new form of socialism has again arisen. This '"new socialism" still has a single solution to Australia's problems. There is still a "capitalism" of exploitation and oppression, only this time the controllers of this regime are male, white and often Christian, those oppressed are indigenous Australians, gays, women and transgender people. Just as economic socialism sought to destroy the wealthy so "new socialism" seeks to tear down "traditional institutions" such as banks, universities, police, and the Catholic church which is seen as a primary purveyor of oppression with its structures of patriarchal male power.

The extensive increase in university courses, such as women's studies, indigenous studies, gender and transgender courses, all target patriarchal white males and organisations like the church whose power must be taken away and transferred to minority groups. Viewing the world through a dishonest prism of power is a typical socialist mechanism. In the case of the church it ignores the church's teachings on charity, forgiveness and the equality of all people. Further attacks are occurring against "binary thinking", that is organisations or individuals who are not accepting of the "modern" idea that gender is fluid and ranges across a wide spectrum of positions.

Catholics who hold that gender is "male and female" and that changes of gender are not in the best interests of the individuals concerned are now labelled as "culturally and socially" backward, with agendas that are concerned with control, oppression and dominance. The scientific proof of XY chromosomes and the great concern of Psychologists regarding sex assignment surgery is of no consequence. The teaching of the church that marriage is between a man and a woman, with the hopeful promise of the creation of a new family belongs to something others are keen to label as "old Catholicism."

Catholicism is entering a vital new struggle where the assertion that gender, like race is considered nothing more than a cultural construct. The church has at this stage blindly and recklessly ignored these new forms of socialism. The penetration into young Australians through mainstream universities ensures that this form of socialism has dramatically taken root amongst young Australians. The support for sexual re-assignment surgery is overwhelmingly supported by under 35-year-old Australians. The indifference of the medical profession to the psychological impact of such surgery is also concerning.

The response of the church to these developments has been insubstantial. We have made no comment on the destruction that such ideas inflict upon individuals, families and wider society. The wellbeing of our society must remain a central Catholic concern, to ignore these new developments including substantial penetration into Catholic schools is a dereliction of Christ's call to transform society into a domain that continues to strengthen and champion the relationship between men and women, the vital life of the family and the happiness and welfare of children. In all these areas we have become dangerously timid.

(IX) A SOCIETY OF TRIBES

The idea that human beings can be improved through selective breeding is almost as old as humanity itself. Plato advanced the idea within his philosophy as early as 400 B.C, yet the modern form of 'eugenics' really came to the fore in the early twentieth century.

Eugenics encouraged individuals deemed 'fit' to reproduce to do so with other selected individuals. On the negative side marriage prohibitions and forced sterilisations were directed at those deemed unfit, usually those with physical or mental disabilities, criminals, deviants and members of disfavoured minority groups.

Perhaps its most brutal expression was practised in Nazi Germany, yet countries as diverse as the United States, Canada, Sweden, India and Mexico have all had policies of forced sterilization for certain groups at different times during the twentieth century. Modern forms of eugenics are alive and well in our day, particularly in the high abortion rates for children diagnosed with downs syndrome and the preference of some cultural groups to desire the birth of sons over daughters. In most cultures, it is the church that has stood alone in its advocacy for the value and preciousness of all life, regardless of abilities, cultures or parental preference.

Americans have rightly held the statement of Dr

Martin Luther King in the 1960's as a high watermark for the ideal and equality of all:

> "I have a dream that my four little children will one day live in a nation where they will not be judged by the colour of their skin, but by the content of their character".

King, a Christian pastor was heavily influenced by the teachings of St Paul who wrote in Galatians 3.28:

> "There is no longer male and female, for you are all one in Christ Jesus".

The ideas and the teachings of the Catholic church are now again in modern Australia under intense challenge and disregard.

The inclusion of mandatory Indigenous studies courses at Australian universities has now moved to a new call for 'Whiteness studies' in my old alma mater Melbourne university. The Oxford university research encyclopedia describes whiteness studies within its true intensions:

> "A growing field of scholarship whose aim is to reveal the invisible structures that produce white supremacy and privilege. Critical whiteness studies presume a certain condition of racism that is connected to white supremacy. Such courses call for white students to admit their complicity in racism, colonialism and the oppression of others".

Again, the Catholic church seems oblivious to the doctrinal mess that young Australians are now subjected. In many cases the underlying confusion of our cultural and academic environment is aided by Bishops who have little positive to say about Australian democracy and society and who speak only in negative teams about indigenous oppression, cruel border protection measures and abuse of the Australian environment. These Catholic leaders bring nothing to the table in terms of joy, pride in Australia or respect for our institutions.

The results continue to be schizophrenic, many people remain desperate to come to our shores because of the freedom, equality and democratic life that we enjoy, yet our own home-grown young Australians are depressed, bored and hopeless for the future.

In our current expression of Australian Catholicism, we are largely silent about the beauties of our nation, the freedoms we enjoy and our great future together.

As Catholic Bishops continue to share nothing of their love of our nation is it really surprising so many Catholics are leaving their congregations. If we have nothing good, positive and wonderful to say about ourselves, can this in any way be called leadership?

Perhaps Jesus himself had something to say about our current situation.

> "It is inevitable that stumbling blocks will come, but woe to the one through whom they come. It would be better for him to have a

> millstone hung around his neck and be thrown into the sea than to cause one of these little ones to stumble" (Luke 17.2).

The stupidity of our intellectual life was on cringeworthy display during the 2016 Brisbane Writers Festival. The American author Lionel Shriver gave an address on the issue of "cultural appropriation". Her central tenet was that writers and novelists must be free to write about the situations of others even if not belonging to that particular group themselves. It would seem a rational position that a white writer could create a character and a story with reference to the life of a black person, or an Asian person or a Russian person, that's what fiction writers are enjoined to do. The desolate and sterile response of a number of Australian commentators displays how poor our intellectual life has become.

An example of this thinking came from the Australian commentator Yassim Abdel-Magied who is hostile to the practice of writing in the voice of someone you are not.

> "She noted 'I can't speak for the LGBTQI community, those who are neuro-different or people with disabilities, but that's also the point, I don't speak for them and should allow for their voices and experiences to be heard and legitimised'."

The camouflage indignation of such views in a fake

morality allows Abdel-Magied to finally move to the core of her hostilities which is all about oppression, racism and lack of freedom in Australian society.

> "The kind of disrespect for others infused in the comments of Lionel Shriver is the same force that sees people vote for Pauline Hanson. It's the reason our first peoples are still fighting for recognition and it's the reason we still stomach offshore detention with prejudice, hate and genocide."

In the face of this idiocy and senselessness the Catholic church has again said nothing. If we allow authors and Australian society to be trashed in this way, in what ways are Catholics to have a voice or to defend the beauty of our own society and the colossal benefits to those who live here.

If the Catholic church will not oppose the view that suggests we may not write about or cannot know the lives of others then we are finished as a society. What will Catholicism be; a church that stood by silently, afraid of encroaching on the territory of others for fear that we may be called out as racist, homophobic or culturally elite? When Australia becomes a nation of cultural eugenics and tribalism to what will the universal church point towards. We are all one in Christ will be long gone!

SECTION II

UNDERSTANDING AUTHENTIC MISSION

(I) AUTHENTIC MISSION – INTELLIGENT CONFRONTATION

The Catholic church cannot flourish or prosper if it adopts a future based on withdrawal (The Benedict Option) or assimilation (The Club-Church Model). Both of these responses are forms of capitulation, the Benedict option accepts abandonment of future societies to their own devices and the club-church model concedes that the Gospel of Christ has no power to change current or future societies without adaption of fundamental aspects of Christ's message.

Such resignation and fearful thinking have never before being so prevalent in Catholic sentiment. At its most serious it abandons the Holy Spirit and the fundamental Christian idea that God has plans and purposes for humanity that go beyond the difficulties of current or future generations.

> "Teach them to observe all that I have commanded and behold I am with you always, even to the end of the age" (Matthew 28.20).

This statement of Jesus seems to have been forgotten in the modern church.

The church has never been about survival, its fundamental historical task and mission is to the transformation of society.

> "These things are written so that you may believe that Jesus is the Christ, the Son of God and that by believing you may have life in his name" (John 20.31).

The actions and mission of Jesus is intimately tired up with the salvation of humanity not the comfort or survival of the church. As a result of this Catholic self-understanding, regarding its mission and purpose, there has always been a clash of values between the church and the world. Catholics have never belonged to the world, nor were they meant to.

Within the ancient Roman world, full participation in the life of society was considered the highest duty. For Romans there was no greater good than citizenship which implied both loyalty and action is support of the state. From its inception the church has always challenged the ideology of host societies. In Roman times the Christian teaching that sexual activity was permissible only within marriage, was an implicit condemnation of the ostentatious hedonism of Roman life. Christianity rejected Roman law in its complete condemnation of Abortion. In Roman families every father had the right to decide if a newborn child lived or died. The church also departed from Roman law by allowing marriage between free people and slaves, subtly ensuring a radical reworking of the Roman practice of slavery. From the beginning the church has challenged and contented with practices it found unacceptable in host societies.

Perhaps the most serious and dramatic conflict with the Roman state arose from the Christian's practice of refusing to worship or acknowledge the state tradition of emperor worship. Increasingly, emperors were regarded as "Sons of God" a title Christians considered as belonging exclusively to Jesus. Whilst these worship requirements of the state were quite minimal (offering small amounts of incense to state Gods) by withholding this expression of state loyalty, the church proposed herself as an alternative to the state in both public and private domains. Perhaps the 2nd century, Gloria, a Catholic psalm which is still central to the modern mass sums up this viewpoint sharply.

> Glory to God in the highest,
>
> And peace to his people on earth
>
> Lord God, heavenly King, Almighty God and father, we
>
> Worship you, we give you thanks, we praise you for your glory.
>
> Lord Jesus Christ, only son of the Father, Lord God, Lamb of God
>
> You take away the sins of the world, have mercy on us;
>
> You are seated at the right hand of the Father; receive our prayer
>
> For you alone are the Holy one
>
> You alone are the Lord

You alone are the most high, Jesus Christ

With the Holy Spirit

In the glory of God, the Father, Amen.

As can be seen from the Gloria, all other expressions of God, society, the good life, riches or private options are subjected to the will of Jesus and of his church. Naturally, such a strong expression of Catholic life, worship and society has been seen as a serious challenge to most societies throughout history.

Monarchies, dictators, communists, oligarchs, democracies, theocracies, fascists and recently secularists have all held reservations about the Catholic church. Many have engaged in forms of suppression, often leading to persecution, murder, destruction of Catholic buildings but most seriously, eradication of their schools, places of worship and theology.

For Catholics resistance and challenge to secular authority has always been an integral part of the life of the faith from Roman times through to the current day. Whilst there are many expressions of Christian "witness" the most profound for Catholics has always been the martyr, those prepared to reject conforming to ideas and values that trample on fidelity to Christ and his call to love of God and neighbour, even to the point of losing their lives.

Martyrdom is never actively sought for itself, but can be an outcome of holding a position that for Catholics cannot be ignored or rejected. The two great English martyrs', Thomas More and John Fisher were killed for not condoning King Henry VIII's divorce and re-marriage, they resisted both the rejection of his first marriage but also his subsequent attempt to subordinate the church to himself.

In modern times, secular and totalitarian regimes such as communist China do not demand worship in state churches, but they do demand Catholics compromise their morals, their belief in human dignity and freedom of speech and their commitment to spreading the Christian message. They care little for what believers do in private but criminalise social, public and internet advocacy for Catholicism.

In the Australian context, the church's teachings of respecting human life and traditional marriage have been abandoned in both state and federal legislation changes. The response of the church must be one of Authentic Mission, speaking the truth without fear, guarding Catholic rights but also preparing to face the consequences of such actions.

In my view, one of the unmatched examples of "Authentic Mission" took place in Berlin, in the life and actions of Monsignor Bernhard Lichtenberg and his resistance to Nazi Germany in the 1930-1940's. Monsignor Lichtenburg believed it was his duty to defend the faith publicly whenever it was attacked or mocked. He spoke out boldly particularly against Nazi attempts to close down Catholic schools, he wrote and spoke consistently about his belief that "where there is only one single Catholic child, there will also be Catholic religious education."

In 1931 as parish priest of St Hedwig's, Berlin, Lichtenberg took the responsibility of prohibiting Nazi party members from receiving the Sacraments. He wrote and spoke relentlessly against Nazi sterilisation laws affecting the handicapped, both German and Non-German, Lichtenberg always wrote directly to the Nazi party officials concerned including Reich Minister Wilhelm Frick who became increasingly annoyed "the Reich government is not going to tolerate such sabotage of Reich laws, which are binding on everyone in the state, including members of the Catholic church."

Lichtenburg also engaged in correspondence with Herman Goering, on the excessive use of punishment in concentration camps, he was not only concerned with Catholic prisoners but wrote in support of social democrats, communists and Jewish internees.

In November of 1938, following the Kristallnacht programs, Lichtenburg began daily public prayers for Jewish Germans and pressured many Catholic organisations to provide paid work for Jews who lost their business or income under Nazi regulations.

Monsignor Bernard Lichtenberg was in confrontation with National socialism over a wide range of issues, yet these were never from a narrow focus on Catholic legal rights but rather from a wider Catholic world view. Lichtenburg opposed the elimination of religious education from schools, the prohibition against sacraments, the secularization of marriage, the deliberate killing of allegedly unworthy life and the persecution of Jews. He noted:

> "I oppose all these things because it goes against the chief rule of Christianity, you should love thy neighbour as you love yourself and I consider the Jews also my neighbours who have immortally created souls in the image and likeliness of God."

In August of 1941 Bernard Lichtenberg was arrested after complaints from two young protestant students who were upset after hearing Lichtenburg publicly pray for Jews. During his interrogation Nazi questioners noted that Lichtenburg had scribbled many condemnatory comments in a copy of Hitler's "Mein Kampf". Lichtenburg noted:

> "I do not consider Hitler a prophet sent by God. The national socialist ideology is incompatible with the teaching and commands of the Catholic church."

Lichtenberg was never to enjoy freedom again in life. He was moved between a number of work camps, where he endured harsh treatment. Lichtenburg was finally sentenced to imprisonment at Dachau concentration camp in 1943 on the charge of endangering public safety. He died on October 28, 1943 whilst awaiting transportation to Dachau. Through his ministry to those who suffered under

National socialism, Lichtenberg made the conscious choice to confront world views that inhibit freedom of thoughts, speech and religious practice, it is for Australian Catholics to do likewise.

(II) NO MISSION – NO LIFE

The Catholic church has ground to a halt in Australia because it does no mission. Priests and parishes occasionally talk about mission, but most Catholic have no idea what it actually means. Almost always our "mission endeavours" are channelled into the Catholic school system and go no further than attempting to get more school parents to bring their families and kids to church.

This has been a huge failure and as almost every parishioner in Australia has seen there is a substantial disconnection between sending your child to a Catholic school and being a faithful, practicing Catholic. Catholic schools might very well be mission opportunities but let's not imagine that the work required to develop and sustain the faith can be done – or is being done in Catholic schools.

The truth is Catholic schools have little to do with the faith in modern Australia. I am not suggesting we abandon them, just place them in a proper context. They do not produce faithful Catholics for the future, and we need a wider and deeper understanding of what we are doing in mission.

So, let's begin with what mission is not! Mission is not "talking" to our fellow Australians about Jesus! Almost always we associate this model with strange individuals who annoy people outside of railway stations or who come knocking on your door at inconvenient times. This type of mission is counter-productive, it discredits the faith, it causes our fellow Australians to consider us as "crazies" and its strike rate is virtually zero.

In modern Australia, we need some fundamental layers of action before mission can begin, most importantly you need credibility and skin in the game, that means you have to be known as reasonable, credible and honest people who have a record of success, at least in a few small areas. So, here's the problem – what has your parish done in the past which will layer some credibility over your desire to do "mission work" – again, in brutal honesty, most parishes are known for very little in their wider communities – most are mass centres, little clubs with signs on the door that tell us the mass times. So, let's not confuse coming to mass with doing mission – what is your parish known for in the local area, this is the platform for mission – not your mass times!

If we are honest about our previous experience of mission, we can see how hard it is to actually get started, let's look at a few attitude and psychological changes that Catholics might need to make if they are to undertake effective, lasting mission.

The Key Thing – Passion

Catholics who seek to do mission in local areas need to realise and acknowledge the value of other people's time. Priests and Catholic lay leaders who think that going through the motions is ok, that their presence in the parish is worth the collection money, that just being the appointed leader is enough, are doing damage to the church and their priestly life.

Tired, broken, bored, cynical or de-motivated priests or laity should not be anywhere near leadership roles in mission. Those involved in mission need to understand clearly that people are trading a significant amount of their valuable time – both for those undertaking the mission and those who are to be challenged by it. Those involved in mission need to understand this – mission is the realm of the passionate. If you are not able to recognise this, be supportive in other ways but don't be caught up in blocking, slowing or undermining those who seek to begin new initiatives.

Mission is Painful and Costly

People who begin fitness programs after many years of absence from physical activity are usually in for a great shock. The road is difficult, painful, tiring and sweaty. The vast majority of those who begin training after long layoffs are at increased risk of injury, most people cease training in a short space of time. The goal of getting fit is a wonderful desire, but the achievement of that goal is a long way off.

The same is true for those commencing mission. Adapting to new stresses is the only way forward. If your parish offers masses, fill these then add another. If you offer a young mum's group get this pulsating and then add another. In "mission thinking" you control the size, depth and passion of your parish but first you must be excellent at what you already do. I travel to many parishes, what I always find, is broken or non-functioning microphones, lights that barely provide enough light, no readers, TV, projectors, screens, musical instruments that don't work, stained carpets, broken tiles, locked doors and unopened car parks. Is this serious? Yes, it is, parishes that can't get the basics right cannot do mission. If you are unprofessional in your current presentation do you really imagine people are queuing up to join you? Shoddy, lazy, half-baked operations are the norm in every diocese – decline is their ongoing journey. Getting fit will cost you – so does mission.

Mission is Method

Humans are designed to see patterns, sequences and order in all that we do. We live our lives by these systems, most of us eat the same breakfast, use the same toothpaste, buy and wear brands that are familiar to us. We are noted for complaining when our systems don't work, or somebody changes a timetable or the aisle in the supermarket. The truth is all of these systems are necessary for us to do things well, efficiently, with reduced cost and effort. When we are faced with uncertainty or patterns we don't understand, we are usually anxious or hesitant until we are able to clearly see the path to take or the best way of doing a new skill or undertaking.

The same is true in mission, often the greatest mistake in mission are due to a "scattergun philosophy" – we try to be "all things to all people", we undertake immense programs of mission in the hope that one or two things might stick. There are always a thousand suggestions or variations to doing or achieving something – almost always these are unhelpful. The famous Test cricketer Shane Warne was noted at the start of each new season for announcing he had discovered a new "mystery ball" during the offseason – his intention was to sow confusion and hesitancy into his opponent – of course he had done no such thing – a cricket ball can spin left or right or go straight. Batsman who failed to realise this were invariably confused as they looked for additional and more complex bowling – no doubt they saw what they wanted to!

The truth in mission is that it is much easier and makes more sense to connect and combine one or two simple ideas, do this well, allowing everyone in your parish/leadership group to see and understand the pattern, goal and outcome. Mission is not meant to be complex – simple patterns and behaviours from everyone gives it the best chance to work.

Doubt is Normal

In whatever human venture you undertake to commence, there will be people who will tell you it's not possible, it can't work, it's a waste of time and money. Often it will be your own inner voice that is also keen to add to all the reasons things are impossible.

When you seek to start mission, you will hear these reasons both internal and external. You will need to make a conscious effort to understand them and have good reasons for rejecting them. If you cannot clearly deal with internal doubt and external rumblings then you are unlikely to commence mission and the work you do commence is likely to be stilted or underdone. The easiest words in our language are "I told you so". Those who undertake to do any mission need to clearly express to those involved, what these complaints, worries, concerns will look and sound like and that they need to be tamed. Mission teams must understand what the opposition will say and how to "tame" them – if you image this is not going to happen then you will fall into a black hole of worry and doubt yourself. Doubt is normal, the mission of the church is given by the Holy Spirit and that casts out fear and doubt. This is a powerful truth.

Sometimes in the Catholic church we can be slow to adapt and change, we like the known and familiar, mission is uncomfortable and without guaranteed results. Nevertheless, if we are without mission we are ultimately without life in our church. Our ability as humans are God given and central to these abilities is adaptation and the ability to change direction. As God requires this of us in our personal lives so he requires this also in his church. It is through God-given mission that our future is assured but we as God's partners need to commence the walk!

There is one other thing to remember:

> We do mission for others; we do this not for ourselves but to transform the world. "Go and make disciples of all Nations" (Matthew 28, 19-20).

(III) THE ESSENTIAL DIFFERENCE OF AUTHENTIC THEOLOGY

There should be no doubt in the minds of the twenty-first century Catholic that we have regressed in time to be living again in the third century. Whilst the third century is largely unknown to the modern Catholic a quick overview shows a series of profound similarities and dangers, particularly in the relationship between the church and the state.

The third century was overwhelmingly a plural and polytheist society. It was assumed as a matter of common sense that there were many Gods with specific deities linked to various cities. Polytheism and the notion of a happy 'collection of citizens' went hand in hand. Symmachus, prefect of Rome, summed this view up succinctly:

> "Everyone has his own customs, his own religious practices, the divine mind has assigned different cities, different religions to be their guardians. We ought to keep faith with our forefathers who followed their forefathers and were blessed in doing so."

As a devoted polytheist the Roman Emperor Diocletian felt exactly the same. It was his duty to protect the diversified nature of the Gods and to halt the claim of Lordship to one individual called Christ.

As the church increasingly developed throughout the empire with an identifiable leadership, Diocletian initiated what would be known to Christians as the great persecution. This oppression singled out the Christian leadership for attack. Bishops and Clergy were arrested and forced to sacrifice to the pagan Gods striking at a fundamental understanding of Catholicism. "He who sacrifices to any God, other than the Lord alone, shall be utterly destroyed" (Exodus 22.20).

Catholicism formed from its inception a society within a society whilst obedient to the state in a passive way, it was noted that criminals were virtually unknown amongst their numbers and that they cared for their own poor rather than seeing them become a state problem.

The most serious disconnection with the state was over the cult of emperor worship, where emperors were exalted as Sons of God, such a designation was a fundamental affront to Catholic loyalty to Christ and resulted in the wide perception that Catholics were a separate association with an allegiance outside of the host society. Thus, the situation the modern Catholic church is experiencing is not new, indeed, Catholics have always been outsiders and have intrinsically described themselves on terms that highlighted their opposition to their host community.

Present day Catholics have powerful reasons for understanding the unpredictable and autocratic nature of most forms of state and national government.

Undeniably the twentieth century and the early decades of the twenty-first have become the unrivalled centuries for Catholic persecution, discrimination and martyrdom. More Catholics and Orthodox Christians have died for their faith in a 120-year period than the first three centuries following Christs crucifixion. The ordeal of Catholics and Orthodox believers under Stalin, Mao, Castro, the Ottomans, Hitler and a host of other communists and socialists make the persecution of the early church appear mild and humane.

The "outsider" nature of the faith is found centrally in the theology of Christ himself, the early church and for all Christians who understand the fundamental "otherness" of Catholic life. It is no wonder the church in the modern world cannot understand mission or seeks to either hide from the world or adapt itself to it. The theology of a church of "Authentic Mission" that seeks to intelligently confront and challenge the world is a church that recognises its own transformation and the transformation of the world rests utterly on its otherness and differences. Catholics do not belong to the world but are called to be "Alter Christus" those who take up their cross. The Christ who is incarnate, enters the Garden of Gethsemane and then fulfils his mission in Calvary, is not an individual who belongs to this world. He dies for it and in that moment transforms it to a new purpose and reality. Because of our Catholic baptism into his resurrection, Catholics are called to carry the grief and burden of others to union with Christ. "Bare one another's burdens and so fulfil the law of Christ" (Galatians 6.2).

The modern Australian church is called to do this, Authentic Mission implies a Catholic who chooses to say to the world "Here I am" (Is 6.8) and one who follows the example of Christ "I lay down my life for the sheep and no none takes it from me but I lay it down of my own accord" (John. 10.15, 18).

Mother Maria Skobtsova at Ravensbruck and Max Kolbe at Auschwitz who both gave their lives in exchange for others can affirm "that greater love has no man than he lay down his life for his friends." The lives of these two martyrs are the lives of individuals who are "beyond this world" and have transformed their own lives into one with Christ. This is the task of Australian Catholics. We cannot be just a social justice church or a welfare provider, this is not the essential nature of Catholicism, yes, we can do good work but overwhelmingly, we are to be known as confronting our world, socially, politically, economically but above all with our self-offering and transfiguration into the life of Christ. That is the ultimate confrontation to our world.

Whether we are called to die outwardly for Christ, in the arena, the gas chambers or the prison camp, depends mostly on external factors, what does depend directly on us, as Catholics in the world is our confrontation with its values, practices and behaviours. This is the basis of taking up our cross daily. To be a practicing Catholic is centrally to do with attending mass regularly, but it also requires an action, a confrontation with ourselves which highlights the centrality of Christs death and resurrection in our lives. If this does not lead to a confrontation with the world, then our transfiguration is but a partial journey. The importance of this confrontation is highlighted by St Paul who notes that his life is formed by "dying each day" (I Corinthians 15.31).

Catholics have always made a distinction between the outward martyrdom of some Catholics and the inner martyrdom of conscience, undertaken by all Catholics. The martyrdom of "all Catholics" is centrally a martyrdom of small sacrifice, yet, it is always based on not conforming to the world.

The future of Australian Catholicism does not rest on conforming to the values of our society but in the example of the English martyrs John Fisher and Thomas More who both gave their lives for the faith but not before that had refused to conform to the values of the world and its emphasis on human and political solutions.

Unfortunately, Australian Catholicism is currently a faith that has lost its Joy. Not surprisingly when a church looks for rewards and prestige gained from its conformity to the world's values. Rewards may well be given but they will always be temporary and given with reservation. True Joy in the faith is always to be found in conforming with Christ but that is first dependent on not being seduced by the world which chokes and suffocates:

> "when trouble or persecution comes because of the word, he quickly falls away. The seed among the thorns is the one who hears the word, but the worries of this world choke the word and it becomes unfaithful" (Matthew 13.22).

(IV) AUTHENTIC MISSION IN ACTION

Overwhelmingly, the most common experience of Australian priests, parishes and diocese is one of overwork, hackneyed originality and shortness of funds. In truth, we are in survival mode, few parishes or diocese have any growth or effective plans for the future years.

Most Australian Catholics no longer know what mission is, which they hopelessly confuse with social justice. A downhill spiral is evident in the practice of merging parishes, stretching priests as pastors to a number of communities and importing overseas priests to plug gaps. None of this has halted the general decline, indeed frustrations at not having sufficient parish pastoral care is increasing, along with often hastening decline in the parishes that no longer have a resident priest living in the nearby presbytery.

A more adverse message to parish culture, history and future hope is hard to imagine than deeming a centre unworthy of having its own priest. This is not intentionally the message of the diocese to such parishes but the "subconscious" on the ground feeling is usually one of abandonment and inevitable decline.

Recently, I encountered the extreme outcomes of this system whilst on holiday in France. An 87-year-old priest, in charge of ten centres, with no help, each village church receiving a daily mass and pastoral care on a ten-day cycle. If we do not change and do mission soon, we risk joining Anglican and other protestant group whose critical mass of parishioners is unable to develop new growth. Catholic decline in previously vibrant Catholic nations such as France, the Netherlands, Portugal, Spain and even Italy are a severe reminder of a bleak future without action.

How can we transform our circumstances in Australia? Firstly, it needs to be noted that mission is not easy, in reality it is hard work, mostly concerned with error and failure. We need to get used to this common experience of lack of success and harness the ability to never give up and start again.

Success only comes when we develop an unyielding attitude to our failures and errors. In truth, most Australian parishes have never tried mission, fear of failure ensures that we continue to do what we have always done, in a mistaken belief that things will change. As of now, things haven't improved by doing more of the same.

A central dimension of mission psychology is to move away from the idea that the exclusive role of the priest or parish is about getting new people to join – yes, mission churches expect that to be an outcome but not because you are offering programs, progressive ideas, extra masses or more prayer groups. Underlying mission is the critical idea that mission is Catholic culture in action, mission is what you do, but you are not "selling" programs, services, bible studies or anything else. Mission involves "living" and expressing your Catholic culture and values.

An illustration may be helpful. Let's imagine your church identifies and decides to support a number of unmarried/single young parents in your area. Prior to initiating any food relief, help with the children, tutoring or any other practical initiative, you must emphasise and stress the Catholic value that you wish to give prominence to. In this case, we are a church that values family life, we support young families (regardless of past circumstances) we are a community that "lives family life" and is prepared to put our time, efforts and finances behind our words. The point of this emphasis is not only for the young family in question, but it is a didactic experience for both parishioners and those outside your community.

You must be able to highlight and commend family life from what you are doing with local families, you must be seen and known as the pro-young family church. And, you must be regularly defending what you do and why, in local magazines, in flyers, in community forums – this is not advertising, it is much deeper projection of your culture onto your local area.

It is not important, whether the family in question comes to mass (hopefully they will) but that is not our primary objective. Our purpose is not only to affect their lives but to transform the lives of our community, to establish our unique Catholic value in our society. We are the people who stand for family, that is our central value and as a bi-product, without condemnation we are also saying, we support marriage, we support two parent families, we recognise the value of fathers in family life.

We must be prepared to say, this is what our actions and deeds are pointing to. This is the basis of all mission, transformation of the world. Unfortunately, we have forgotten this central understanding and sidetracked our energies into a survival model, which only makes statements about how wonderful and caring we are.

Mission is living our culture and values, radically different to our local communities, which often say that individual success is the highest human achievement. All mission is founded as Christ's words "For God did not send his Son into the world to condemn the world but to save the world through him" (John 3.17).

The method of Authentic Mission

Form Cadres

In its best formation and expression, the Catholic parish is an influential and powerful representation of the Christian life. The average Australian parish is somewhere between 3-4 hundred to a thousand members. In practice this should mean a community in which strong relationships between members and their priests and ministry teams can develop. The truth is often different, where parishioners don't know each other, priests can remain aloof or distant and the nature of the parish is one of disconnection. A parish wishing to undertake mission cannot be like this.

A mission orientated parish must be tightly meshed, careful to ensure the fullest communication and involvement of all members and one that develops a distinct personality. In military jargon, this is called the command climate and reflects the tone of the commander. All football coaches, CEOS's, prime ministers and yes priests must develop this distinct environment, that defines the nature of who you are. I am not talking of parish mission statements but of setting the parish "tone" by knowing each other, learning the personalities, strengths and weaknesses of every person in the parish. A Roman centurion was required to know and communicate with every man in his century. It may well be necessary for mission parishes to establish "centurions" for just this purpose. This is not about pastoral care; this is not about making parishioners "work" for the parish. It is principally about knowing your people so that ideas, area knowledge, skills, connections and communication can be channelled into a comprehensive mission "frequency" for the parish.

When forming cadres for ministry it is important to remember and emphasise that this is not about acquiring the best "outsider" to do this for you. This must be a local project and you use what God has provided. There will always be concerns about what you don't have, the ones who have left and the "talent" that doesn't wish to be involved. Hankering constantly after those who may join at some later stage is wasteful and debilitating of mission. Start with what you have and do not worry about the ones you don't.

In the first few months, the task of the "centurion" is to build knowledge of your people – talk to them about their ideas of mission and begin to select and assemble some mission initiatives that may be undertaken and entrusted to your mission teams (still to be formed). At this stage, the key value is energy. Energy and enthusiasm for possible tasks and verve and determination in individuals who may wish to be involved. If discussions/planning and possible features do not generate vitality and personal animation, store it and move onto the next mission possibility.

Mission is too hard to sustain with half-hearted people. Eventually, your energy must be infectious, travelling through the parish. Don't be concerned about whether a mission proposal will work or not, with the enthusiasm of the Holy Spirit all things are possible. A mission parish is defined and formed by what you do, in the long run perhaps only 1 out of 10 ideas will actually work but without a parish that believes in "taking mission on" then at your parish heart you will be unable to do anything. Mission is a human exercise, success or otherwise is God's gift to us.

During the "collection" period which centrally involves collecting information regarding mission opportunities and the skills and enthusiasm of the parishioners, the priest must be considering the formation of the "mission team". This team should be another "tight group of parishioners" that appear to have a particular "bent" for knowing people and for communicating clearly and simply with parishioners.

Ultimately, this group must have the confidence of the parish priest but equally they must have confidence in their priest. This relationship only develops and grows by doing things together. This may be shared meals and friendly conversation but also requires shared experiences and I would urge some form of challenging training or weekend tasks that can be undertaken together. At base, the mission team is a group of individuals that will need significant trust in each other and some knowledge of how individuals within the team, think, act, react to criticism or evaluate programs. This level of intimacy will take some time to develop and does require time spent together. There can be no shortcuts in the formation of an effective mission team.

Mission in Depth

The brutal truth about Australians parishes is that not much mission actually gets commenced. Most parishes have never discussed the mission possibilities in their local areas. Somehow, over time, we have come to see this as the role of the priest or a function of diocese administrators and agencies. Yet, unequivocally the failure to set about local mission is the origin of

Catholicism's slow descent into irrelevance. Moreover, the mission that is embarked on is usually, short term, involves small members of parishioners and ends up draining and wearing out those who have offered to help. The Authentic approach to mission is focused on undertaking mission in depth, particularly in two important dimensions.

Firstly, Authentic Mission teams must be sufficiently large enough to avoid fatigue and loss of energy. A mission team must be more than 2-3 dedicated parishioners. Indeed, in a standard parish of around 1000 members, 30-40 will be required for the substantial role of developing, planning, initiating, recruiting and evaluating mission projects. The Authentic Mission group is not a program that you buy and roll out, it is a unique, local undertaking with individuals who take on changing and diverse roles. Some may come and go, some may step back after a few months, the working relationship on this team, must be evaluated, changed and reset every few months. Without this extreme flexibility, exhaustion easily takes hold. Commitment to this group is one of short-term bursts. Amongst people who lead busy lives, the feeling of being captured or controlled or unable to escape must be avoided.

Secondly, Authentic Mission in depth must apply to those involved in face to face delivery of a program. This team is the delivery team, the hands-on team, the team charged with a successful accomplishment of the mission project and they also must be largish in number, perhaps twice the size of the planning team. In a manner similar to the planning team people who undertake hands on roles in mission cannot be strangers to one another. This team must be sufficiently familiar with each other to be able to predict each other's reactions, there can be some stressful encounters in project delivery, it is important that members of this delivery team actually like each other, not just be doing duty or putting up with each other. The parish priest has the essential role in this network of ensuring that relationships/friendships are maintained, indeed that the shared work of doing mission, which may be tiring, is still one of joy and a feeling of achievement.

So, what does mission in depth actually look like. Perhaps, your planning team has decided to undertake a particular ministry to a group of young, under-skilled women who live within your parish. To undertake mission to any specific group it is of critical and primary importance that you do not undertake just one project or idea. Resting, the success or failure of your mission idea on just one program usually leads to disappointment and burnout. Mission projects are not expected to be hit or miss. These programs may work, yet, they often have the seeds of desperation about them, particularly if only small numbers of parish members are involved, it is unlikely these members would front up for other mission endeavours in the short term. Mission in depth implies that with sufficient numbers of parish people involved your durability and infrastructure allows you to transform or change as programs unfold. You are in it for the long term but what you commence may well not be what you end up with.

Mission to a section of young under skilled women in your parish could be run across 6 or 7 particular fields, with a focal point on implementing programs that the women themselves respond to and appear interested in.

A basic model might include, cooking classes, help with child minding, establishing a free gym or pilates class, tutoring for children, provision of part time work somewhere in the parish, establishing an excursion or cinema or cultural group meeting on parish premises, language classes, home maintenance or car repairs. The list of potential connections can grow to substantial size, usually 6 or 7 is sufficient but each must be co-ordinated and operated by different small teams of at least 4-5 parishioners.

It is then a case of waiting to see what works well in your area, which facets of the mission is taken up and ensuring that burn out and fatigue are not visible. A parish mission to 20 women in your parish who could benefit from your support indicates to your local community that you are parish that actually engages and develops those amongst whom you live. This is the first stage of mission, energising your own people to "see" and offer local support and ensuring that others "see" you as a tiered community, practical support, strong community life and a spiritual heart that rests on the gift of Christ's life itself.

The function of leadership is crucial at this hands-on phase. Leadership must ensure you do not get bogged down in things that lose momentum and rewards those who are getting on with it. Once mission begins, however small, we cannot draw back from it. This is the second stage of mission, things may fail, end in disappointing fashion, yet mission itself continues in another form. Parishes that undertake Authentic Mission begin to buy into the "naturalism" of mission and its never-ending life. It is no longer "hard work", it becomes like breathing, we no longer think about it, we just do it!

Relentless Planning

In addition to sustained mission in depth, we also must be unyielding in our planning. That means planning never ends. New ideas and possibilities are constantly emerging, evaluation and procedures for acquiring resources, ideas and team members is ongoing. This is a clear indicator that your parish has evolved into one that constantly looks to undertake mission – because your parish, the body of Christ, is no longer able to consider life without mission. Some individuals and sub-groups will be at rest, but the parish is not.

New initiatives, plans, leaders and team members will always be emerging. The Holy Spirit is a busy person and to those whom much is given, much will be expected. This type of parish is at the cutting edge of God' work.

For this reason, I recommend establishing a "command mission centre". This might be a dedicated space in your parish complex, it should clearly outline the undertaking you have commenced, who's involved in leadership, group members, the tasks being undertaken and opportunities for others to join. Additionally, future plans, discussions and avenues for mission should also be openly declared. Parishioners should be encouraged to visit this room, add their ideas and make further suggestions. This room is essential for forming and maintaining the direction of your parish. It also helps you to "confirm" what you have done well in the past and gives hope that future mission opportunities will also go well.

The "tone" of your parish is created and perpetrated by the number of people who involve themselves "psychologically" in the idea and action of mission.

No one can guarantee success, perhaps a parish has nothing but bad luck and failures, nevertheless, this is unimportant. The human dimension of mission is in starting, trying, doing the best you can. The divine aspect is bringing this to fruition, that's God's business not ours.

Authentic Mission is fundamentality peripatetic; we walk with God as Adam did in the garden, and train our people to get stronger. We are encouraging people to carry notebooks, to write down new ideas, to note how something may be done better. All of these ad-hoc plans are a central symbol to your parish, because they indicate the desire of your parish to be mission orientated and to conduct mission no matter who is the parish priest, no matter what the make-up of teams is and no matter what the tasks to be undertaken are. When mission moves to the front of the parish psyche something special is imminent.

Psychological Disposition

Australian culture and attitude of mind is at the beginning of the 21st century significantly risk adverse. There are always lots of reasons why something can't be done, most of these will centre on aspects of insurance, costs, lack of resources, lack of skilled individuals but the most common is always the one that should be easy to overcome but never is, "we have never done this before", "None of our priests has ever asked us to do this before", "I'm not a good speaker" or a "confident person in public" so I won't be able to be involved.

Most of these "people" objections have at their base a funny notion of mission, almost always based on the door knocking, street evangelical model, that is often extremely counterproductive.

So, before you commence mission and as you go through the process you will always need to affirm, what you are not doing, what kinds of stresses a parishioner role will bring and what kind of support you and your mission team will be offering. If you are not prepared to do this continuous psychological framing and inspiration you will find that obstacles, objections, fears and worries will all become much larger, taking on a life of their own and potentially disrupting or crippling the work you are planning to do.

Constant updates on why we are doing something, how proud we are of those involved, how much we appreciate the work and preparation they do, and a little background on all the unseen labour that takes place before mission can commence. Authentic Mission requires a constant layer of clarification of goals, encouragement, rewards and vision of a better future. Mission is a future driven exercise and a way of taking control of your own future and life together.

Too many parishes and priests are content to allow things to happen to them and prefer a quiet and uneventful life. Unfortunately, this is not the life that Christ himself promised his followers, opposition, family dissentions, loss of friends, self-doubt, mistakes and martyrdom are firmly on the list of possibilities. If we add a society that has reached a level of contentedness and with a disposition that incessantly calls to government or other authorities to do things, then it should be expected that mission initiatives can be met with a view centred on "why should we have to do this?" The answer is Christ's response to his disciples prior to the feeding of the 5000, "you give them something to eat!" (Mark 6.37).

I am reminded of what the first American

President George Washington wrote to congress during the American War of Independence "Men who are familiarised with risk meet it without shrinking; whereas those unused to service often see danger, where no danger is".

Authentic Mission needs sustained positive messaging and perpetual preparation. The goal is always to strengthen the psyche and faith of all those involved in mission. It can be an arduous and unrewarding process, especially in the early stages. Parish priests and leaders must ensure that psychologically the whole parish has details of small wins and that these small triumphs can be built into a strong vision of future success.

Take nothing for granted, negative vibes and fears will surface even amongst the strongest individuals, encouragement, preparation and vision of future success must be at the forefront of the minds of all those who live within a mission orientated parish.

Talk Don't Email

Authentic Mission is founded on walking and talking. Mission is a peripatetic, moving feast. Its starting point, its completion and everything in between is based on talking and listening to your people. To do that you must be able to see the subtle and gradual messages that are given to you whilst they are undertaking mission. In similar mode to a good military leader you must be always at the front line to gauge levels of confidence, enthusiasm or layers of fear or confusion. You can only do this if you turn up at the coal face and ask people about what they are doing and why. It is important that you constantly ask your teams to explain or describe their actions in significant depth.

The leadership and the wider team must be able to grasp these deep layers and to immerse yourself in understanding complexities. If leaders and team members don't understand the tactics in play, the success and failures and the effort required to undertake mission work, just how will a leader provide insight, wisdom and growth? You cannot sustain mission if you stay in your office and talk to your teams on email. Visit, walk with them, understand and immerse yourself in their issues, without this, mission cannot begin with intensity and it surely cannot change lives.

At all times it is essential for all concerned to make sure that mission activity is performed with competence. People know when a task is performed at rubbish levels and they will stop coming. All team members must ensure that the basics are done well. That means the lights go on early, the rooms are clean, the toilets are working, the full team is ready to operate 20-30 minutes before commencement. There can be no amateur hour, you do not have to be brilliant at your job but you do have to master it.

This applies especially to leaders, analyse yourself, identify weakness and note keenly areas that you need to improve upon. If you are unwilling to discipline yourself to check and correct your own effort, do you really expect others will magically do it for the mission activity? The desire to improve will be noticed. Authentic Mission is mostly caught not taught.

The aim of Authentic Mission is to draw new people to Catholicism, from the integrity of the mission and life we lead together. Yet, this is inseparable from standing up for those values in tough times. There cannot be a do as I say not as I do in mission leadership.

Authentic Mission is also formed around caring, but not a sloppy, patronising or emotional form of caring that equates itself with agreement or popularity. The 36th President of the United States, Theodore Roosevelt summed up the discipline of real compassion:

> "Nobody cares how much you know, until they know how much you care."

This means knowing the goals and hopes of your people, it means knowing how they learn best, it means knowing what their best self wants to achieve and be. Without these things you know nothing at depth, and you will be unable to discipline or speak bluntly when performance goes astray.

It is fundamental to leadership to be without favouritism. Those you like, or those who like you invariably make poor associates. Above all, you must value persistence, determination and a never give up attitude. Those who cross personal and social boundaries will distort their leadership. Perhaps the most common fault of leadership is found in surrendering authority through friendship. In Authentic Mission, leadership is found in instructing, teaching, suggesting and ultimately in directing. You cannot do this to your friends.

Finally, Authentic Mission is based on Catholic values and convictions. More than determination, or persistence your mission must be formed by Catholic values. Yet, very definitely these are distinctive and unique. It might be the case that in the immersion with local secular principles or conventions some parishioners may have forgotten what is unique about Catholic culture and ethics. That's ok, be prepared to re-teach these things, we have much to be proud of in our history. It has 2000 years of success and benefit. In Authentic Mission we affirm, reform and activate our values for a new and desperately needy society. Be proud to be Catholic. God has charged his church with the transformation of the world and nothing is more important than this.

Managing Opposition

The vast majority of the human race is not made up of self-motivated, energised individuals prepared to take on new initiatives or looking to making a difference in society or even their local area. Despite our national stereotypes about go-getting, fearless and enthusiastic Australians, the truth lies closer to a nervous, hesitant and somewhat self-centred society.

Our natural disposition is now one firmly distrusting of politicians, authority figures and Catholic priests! Younger Australians also seem to be floundering in anxiety, high levels of depression and higher levels of suicide. The tendency to join groups and associations is extremely low and declining further.

Nevertheless, this cohort of diffident Australians is still very keen to express viewpoints, criticisms and disparaging comments towards those who are prepared to try new enterprises and ways of doing things. When you seek to commence Authentic Mission in your parish you will absolutely be assailed by some individuals full of negativity, cynicism and doubting comments. Try something new and this will definitely happen. It is a vital component of mission that these comments, untruths, unconvinced and mistrustful arguments be brought into the open and challenged.

It is vital for long term mission and the life and death of your locally chosen tasks, that you assign some individuals to report the health of these initiatives. What does the wider parish make of them? What are the concerns? And how do these critical individuals suggest other methods or practices may be used. Each initiative should have at least two individuals of discretion and tact who are able to take the wider pulse of the initiative. Reports and feedback given to the various Authentic Mission teams should be written, concise, honest and as far as possible also outline other ways results may be achieved.

These individuals must not be seen as spies but rather creative forces in the completion of initiatives. Essentially, their task is to help control the two factors which always lead to the destruction of new ideas and mission initiatives. Firstly, there will always in some individuals be a lot of emotion, almost all opposition to new ideas is emotional, this has been tried before, other priests have done this, this goes against something I would do, or hoped to do, this is a waste of money. It does not take much for people to find solace in anger, frustration, disappointment and hurt. It is critical that those collecting information are able to identify the emotional context of people's objections and then help them to compartmentalise it – mission should not be destroyed or damaged by emotions, but it can be if they are left un-identified, expressed and then acknowledged within the wider context.

Take note of emotions but always place those who make them within the greater context of the goal of changed parishes, increased parish comradery and the hope for new visions and new parishioners.

Secondly, those taking the barometer of parish viewpoints, must be able to identify and highlight distractions. No, we are not working with all under 35-year-old women, we are only working with 2 of them. Yes, there may be more worthy examples or deserving individuals, yet we have committed and remain focused upon these particular individuals.

It is important, not to let new mission initiatives be distracted into bigger and better things before you have even begun. Start small, maintain focus on limited goals, achieve them, gain knowledge and energy from them and start again.

Do not get so large and complex you are unable to have an early win. This is the key value of Authentic Mission, start small, limit your resources to ensuring some wins and beneficial results, promote these wins, modify your tactics and move on to the next task.

Mission is chaotic and messy; it does not unfold to plan, and it will cause shock and upset to some people. This needs to be explained and understood but it also requires those involved to be single-minded, purposeful and unyielding until a goal is obtained.

When the mission team has concluded that the task is complete, then there is time for review and analysis but not before. Most parishes do not undertake mission because they know it is painful, difficult and messy.

Many parishes that do start Mission are often unable to finish because they are distracted, too quick to change and don't have simple achievable goals. Finish the job for good or bad. If you don't, you have only taught yourself that it is "too hard" for us, and subsequently made it easier to go back to the way things were before.

Above all, mission is energising, do you achieve everything you wish? No, you don't, but you can still grow and develop energy, purpose and a sense of motivation for future endeavours. Mission results are not of primary importance but building energy and persistence for the next one is.

Giving Thanks

Giving public thanks must be constant. Each week in parish life those involved in your mission, the planners, the doers, the receivers, the givers of feedback and those who are tired and sometimes defeated must be thanked. Never forget to do this.

This is a positive expression in the life of your parish and importantly it builds resilience and persistence. All great leaders have been able to identify things that needed changing and making better, but that is not what made them great. Greatness comes from harnessing the energy and passion of those who do not always feel able to give. The request for one more try is where leadership is found. Those who have been thanked understand more of what you require and importantly they understand when things must end. Thanking those involved is the air that surrounds your mission initiative. If you do not thank those involved, you will undervalue their energy and future involvement. Humans that have offered "to do" something are precious and rare. Ultimately, all that we do within Authentic Mission is in the hands of God and yes, we give thanks to him as well. Giving thanks to God and your people tells them indeed that they are "the body of Christ."

Why Mission Fails

Commonly, the instigation of mission and many of its applications end in failure. The truth of mission is that it is overwhelmingly an undertaking that ends in failure. In my experience perhaps only twenty percent of mission activities will come to a successful conclusion. When we undertake new mission, particularly if those involved have not previously engaged in mission, we should expect large doses of failure. All those involved in new mission must be taught to expect failure. Leaders must be prepared for failure and develop strategies that determine adaptations and new paths to success. Failure, disappointment, incompletion and sometimes train wrecks are part of mission.

Nevertheless, there is no reason not to commence mission. Christs central command to his followers is one of mission. "Go and make disciples of all nations" (Matthew 28:19) and we cannot therefore behave as if such a task is not incumbent upon each individual follower of Christ and each community.

Catholics are called fundamentally to be people of mission. The actuality within Australian Catholicism is that we have never been particularly strong at undertaking this command of Christ. Perhaps our current situation of smallish, struggling, fearful and disconnected local communities reflects years of neglect in this area.

There is a number of common reasons why mission

engagement may be slow to commence or not arrive at hoped for outcomes. Undoubtedly, the local parish will be made up of many well-intentioned amateurs and perhaps those who have a vague interest in doing "something" but are not sure what that might be. This is not an excuse for failed mission, that's what God has given the parish and that's what God expects us to work with. People must be trained, taught, encouraged and developed in the "thinking" that makes mission achievable. It's not easy but let's get rid of the first excuse 'my people aren't much good' and get on with the business of their development.

Of much more serious concern, and an attitude that lies at the heart of mission failure is the idea "that father knows best." If parish leaders buy into this notion that "they and they alone" are the experts, mission is in serious jeopardy. Such viewpoints blind leaders to the gifts and skills of others and ensure that initiatives are of narrow dimensions. If your priest or leadership group are the only ones who can run anything then you will ensure that blandness and passivity are at the core of what you do. Being open to other ideas and surrounding yourself with good people gives mission a chance to be varied, appeal widely and perhaps score some wins. Limited owners mean limited goals, risks and outcomes. Poor leaders concern themselves with control and always go nowhere! Good leaders drive, energise and direct outcomes. They don't need to come up with every idea or plan as well.

Catholicism has a particular blind spot in this area.

In many ways we are a church of stiff and inflexible methodology, we are hierarchical, and many individuals derive their credibility and status from a system of order and placement within that system. On occasions our preference is for waiting for decision making to devolve from other levels of the hierarchy, from Bishops, diocesan officials or the local priest.

At one level Authentic Mission seeks to reverse this order, strategic decisions need to be developed and understood locally, in combination of priest and people together, oversite remains with the priest but no one individual can develop an effective local mission strategy. A distant group of diocesan officials who have never visited your parish and don't know the local area have even less likelihood of offering effective strategies. Authentic Mission is largely tactical, requires improvisation, quick decision making and rapid change to mutating developments.

This is the great cause of mission failure. It sticks too tightly to an original plan that isn't working – local spontaneity and confidence in local decisions and understanding is what drives success. Lack of flexibility in delivery and over reliance on a few individuals is the primary cause of mission failure.

Planning is vital to successful mission, yet it is easy to become overly reliant on the plan. Certainly, it should be detailed to an exact and meticulous degree, yet it still must be flexible enough to allow for individual interpretations and understandings to flourish. Mission needs acts of spontaneity, following procedures yet being unable to adjust to changing circumstances often results in boredom, particularly for participants and mission team members. The value and virtues of mission initiatives are found in their enjoyment and energy, delivering these dimensions usually ensures that they are effective and working efficiently. Team members who share their different ways of running a program ensure that mission remains fresh, lively and ever varied.

Building sustainable mission is hard work and new definitions of what success looks like are also relevant. If you had planned and hoped for twenty participants but you find in reality only ten, is this a failure? No ...this is half a success! In most mission initiatives there is plenty to build upon, there is usually no need to completely commence again, just modify and build on the ten you have. Too many Catholics are prone to giving up, too early after commencement. It is important in the early stages of mission to constantly adapt what success looks like. To downsize from twenty to ten requires a different method and plan and when that's done, another interpretation of success.

This is the centrality of what mission looks like, start, adapt, build again, re-start, adapt build again, unless you are prepared to develop and expect teams to foresee and understand mission in this way, then any little failure on the journey is likely to derail your good intentions.

(V) THE ELEPHANT IN THE ROOM – WHAT DOES FATHER DO?

Inquisitive Questioning

Increasingly as Catholic clergy are required to take on more parish centres, schools and administrative burdens the methods and operations of the priest must change.

It is no longer possible for one priest to be the fount of all knowledge. Indeed, clergy who still cling to this level of total jurisdiction over layers of a parish are inevitably facing exhaustion, breakdown and eventual collapse. Moreover, they create in their people dependence and lack of creativity because parishioners quickly learn of limitations and boundaries but rarely hear of possibilities, new beginnings and team endeavours.

In this model parishioners are confronted with a bleak choice, leave all the "work to father" or move somewhere else. I have conducted supply in some parishes where nobody knows where any keys are found and where light switches and microphones can't be operated because "father does all that."

Authentic Mission requires a priest to be operating with greater ingenuity and inquisitiveness than this. A model with the priest as "fount of all knowledge" is not recognising the level of leadership sophistication that is required to oversee the modern Australian parish. Within Authentic Mission the position and function of the priest becomes much more substantial and vital. Additionally, it is my contention that it makes priesthood more seminal and satisfying.

The central transition for a priest beginning to understand mission is operating in an environment of constant questioning and the great questions all priest should be asking their people are what have we overlooked? And what should we do?

The point of such questioning is to encourage your parishioners to be asking the same question of themselves. At the end of every team meeting, parish council or even every mass, priests should insist on receiving at least one hard question. How else will the priest know what his people really think? How else will he encourage others to listen to him if he doesn't listen to them? Good and valuable ideas often come from the most unlikely of sources and young and old are capable of profound insight. Authentic Mission requires a background of creativity and restlessness, clergy create this by constantly asking what have we overlooked? And what should we do next?

Underlying, the inquisitive and questioning priest is another foundational and core outcome. Don't be taken by surprise! There are the two types of distressed and malfunctioning parishes, one is where the priest does everything, nothing changes and the vast majority of parishioners have no stake in the future. The other is the chaotic and floundering parish, which can't seem to hold onto good people and seems constantly subjected to high acts of drama, clash, argument and walkouts. Both of these types of parish are facing collapse because a non-confrontational method of questioning is missing. Never questioning your people or them questioning you will give a priest a quiet life and perhaps the illusion of success. Being constantly surprised by drama will give you a noisy and chaotic parish life, the truth is neither will grow.

A good methodology for questioning is found in a 3-stage formula which ensures you get information; parishioners give and receive feedback and leads to an understanding of a constantly changing future.

(i) How is the initiative going?
(ii) Who needs help – who needs congratulating?
(iii) What next?

You can learn to plan your questions so that they do not just produce criticism and worry. It is the role of the priest to be influential, productive and imaginative. The Catholic life is not tasteless, tawdry or boring. The transformational priest is needed more than ever, it begins with questioning.

Liaison

In the teamwork of an Authentic Mission parish the parish priest is not absent from the key decisions, indeed his oversight roles ensures that he must be intimately involved and charged with the final yes or no in relation to new mission. Nevertheless, once decisions are made and mission teams have been briefed, planning completed and methods expanded, it's time to let the tasked teams get on with it.

Effective and successful decision making is never set and forget. In truth, the decision to undertake an initiative in mission is not the most important decision. The vital and pivotal decisions will all be within the implementation stages. This means that most decisions will be heavily packaged with liaison and connectedness. The unfolding of a new mission will always require adaptation, change and ways of re-starting. This means that clergy decisions can't be imposed, they must grow out of discussions and understanding. Enforced changes to mission goals that are not widely owned will result in the failure of the mission.

In addition, the importance of liaison and communication is integral to ensuring demarcation between groups working on differing aspects of the mission. This serves to reduce conflict and vitally keeps each particular aspect of the mission on maintaining their own inputs and orientation towards either starting, holding or developing their tasks. If you do not listen and communicate with the mission teams the initial decision to commences will often result in confusion and lack of results.

Reach and Tempo

Successful mission is primarily about reach and tempo. The question of how sizeable your mission will be and at what speed you conduct it are two pre-eminent questions. It is a broadly my experience that quickly undertaking mission activities usually stems from incomplete planning and has a high risk of reducing those involved in its implementation to exhaustion. Mission is usually a long-distance running exercise, the paths may disappear, the tracks become saturated by flooding or overgrowth inhibits progress, yet these are normal in long distance mission and should not mean that initiatives have failed or need to be stopped. Considering new ways to reach the target must be considered at all stages of the journey. Undoubtably, financial issues impact on mission activity and often determine how fast a task can be undertaken and what required resources might be needed. Without careful planning, spending can run out of control.

Tempo will usually be determined by both human resources and financial strength. It is important to recognise that many individuals will agree to participate but find that long-term commitment is beyond them. That is a common experience. Volunteers are notorious for often failing to show up to events or to complete them on time. Planning will need to build this reality into the tempo of how expectations may be met in timely fashion without causing friction, disappointment or embarrassment.

Volunteers have a shelf life, an additional reason for ensuring that reach and tempo are kept within manageable and achievable boundaries.

With Volunteers, it is usual for dropout rates of around 30%. Your program cannot be derailed by a failure to not foresee this. Have human reserves ready, be prepared to delay or slow the completion of a program and continue to offer lashings of praise and encouragement.

If you do not encourage or thank your volunteers you will not keep them for long. Yet, I am constantly surprised that volunteers are expected to go on year after year without acknowledgement – importantly, they need to hear of their centrality to the mission undertaking, no matter how small that may be.

Many Australian parishes struggle financially, this is no reason, not to do mission, but it does mean a parsimonious attitude must prevail.

It will be necessary for the planning team to continually reinforce what the expenses are and why future funds may not be available. Those involved in mission initiatives need to know this, it avoids disappointment and disheartening attitudes. There is a difference between frugality and stinginess. People can take pride in mission and accept change or downsizing as long mission leadership teams are viewed as financially trustworthy and openly communicative. Money might be tight but leaders must ensure that some completion occurs without total cost cutting.

Hacking programs to starvation levels after you start only ensures there will be no future contributors to your mission.

Be Pugnacious

Timidity and fearfulness in mission guarantees failure. The vast majority of Catholic mission activities are commenced in a half-hearted manner. Much of the wider parish knows nothing about them, they are not widely talked about and when they fail those involved are saved any embarrassment. Authentic Mission requires boldness; therefore, your mission intention must be displayed before the whole parish community. Whilst mission statements are popular in parishes, in my view, they indicate a parish that has suspended itself from the rough and tumble of Catholic life. Mission statements that speak of seeking to know Jesus in scripture, celebrating him in prayer and praise and being a people of loving service are beautifully sounding but useless and irrelevant.

It is much more substantial and of greater substance to publish your mission objective, what you are doing, who's involved, what difference will you make, what does success look like, what happens if we fail and how much it costs.

When you do this, you are not a parish trying to be faithful, you are "doing" already. It doesn't matter if this works or fails, "to do" is the mission. Publicise your intent in a simple and achievable format and get rid of statements about love, faithfulness and hope. Mission objectives that are not specific and outcomes based are just mumbo-jumbo. Authentic Mission parishes ask the whole parish to know what you are on about in clear and specific language. If you can't do this, you have already sown confusion and risk retreat into business as usual where generally nothing happens.

The first dimension of being pugnacious is to stand up as a parish and declare what you are on about – publicly – hiding mission is valueless, it doesn't encourage ownership, pride or an attitude of doing. Therefore, the priestly role is one of constant coaching, pep talks, public congratulations in newsletters, these are important dimensions of promoting and owning the mission. It is also a leader's responsibility to generate energy and this also is a public modus operandi, your approach must be public and focused. A continuous week by week acknowledge of what your mission is, is an important method for sustaining energy and displaying the key nature of your expectations.

Leadership in many ways cannot be taught, but it can be seen and caught. You are leading your parish when you display energy, reward publicly and highlight the small wins. All of this generates unity, purpose and support in your people. A coach or leader without passion is unlikely to enthuse anyone to join the mission, nor will it sustain the ones you already have. From time to time leaders are required to correct or criticise the manner in which individuals behave or a mission initiative has been conducted. In my experience, there is an unequivocal way this must be done. Praise in public, criticise in private. All criticism must be private, leadership and mission will be injured by public disagreements, frictions develop and the space everybody needs to move, adapt and save face is diminished.

Anger and frustration are normal human emotions and they will be present in a Catholic parish as well. It is certainly important for clergy and other leaders to stand their ground and hold their viewpoints. Nevertheless, criticism that becomes public or are conducted in public don't usually give the room needed for adapting and recovering. Criticism does not mean ravaging or demolishing another's position. Comebacks do happen – allow for them.

Go to press – after the job is done!

Getting your mission initiative into the press is an important outcome, yet it is vital to only do this when you control the story. That is, you know the ending and you are happy for your understanding of the ending to be acknowledged. Mission is a good news story therefore mission activities should reflect on both what you have done and of who you are at heart.

Authentic Mission is not an advertising exercise, it is not about racking up success after success, rather it seeks to provoke a new understanding of how your Catholicism is activated. You don't need press to do that, but it may add to your own view of your community and what others think of you, if the results are also positive and energising.

The great difficulty for Catholic organisations is that many media outlets, including local papers are inclined to bring their own overlay to the Catholic church. Unfortunately, in recent decades we have given media organisations many avenues for criticism and negative comment. Nevertheless, new beginnings bring new opportunities, yet if you initiate press contact with half-finished mission you encourage the media organisations to plug the gaps with their own interpretations for your work or your local history. This should not be a discouragement but a determination to ensure there is a successful story to your initiatives.

Positive energy – positive messages

In the same manner as you deal with the press you must deal with your local community. This is basic respect, say positive things that build and create an energetic culture. Your parishioners and visitors to your parish will pick up on double messages, hidden tensions and flattering words that are not backed up in actions. Importantly, messaging starts locally, in your buildings, with your people, get this right prior to glossy magazines or invitations to stylish Christmas services.

In the early days, you don't need diocesan or

regional approval, use your common sense but get your own initiatives in order. Seeking the guidance of headquarters experts has a sad history of failure and wastage. Small initiatives and small wins are what to look for, not imposed structures that may have worked elsewhere, or which were designed by committee.

Authentic Mission is local mission, it will not necessarily be workable in the parish five kilometres away. You are not them, so discuss, design and initiate something new and unique for your environment operated and owned by your people.

Christ calls us to do mission in our area, that is a unique and special charge given only to you. Overwhelmingly, Authentic Mission is usually small and intimate, your job is to speak to those within your boundaries that have not yet heard of you. If you are not prepared to own and direct your own mission, why would others do it for you? Authentic Mission is different because it works through you, your first step is to get that local initiative airborne, where it takes you is God's business.

SECTION III

AUTHENTIC MISSION IN ACTION A FEW IDEAS TO GET YOU STARTED

(I) THE DIGNITY OF WORK – MISSION ENGAGE

Why

The world of work is the most important mission field in modern Australia and the Catholic Church is utterly absent from it. Why is work so central to mission? Because it is the most basic indicator of who we are as individuals and who we are as a society. To be absent from this sphere of Australian life is to place the church on the margins of society.

The church must have "skin in the game", people are not unintelligent, they know when an organisation is talking at them. The church makes lots of calls to increase welfare, or to increase the unemployment benefit. All well and good but this is not getting people a job. Significant and long-lasting mission is an entirely different enterprise than calling for increased benefits. A genuine understanding of the working world and its centrality to mission requires integrity, persistence, planning, networking and putting your money where your mouth is!

So, let's look at what an accurate understanding of the value of work might look like.

Pope John Paul II in his Encyclical "Laborem Exercens" notes powerfully the essential connection between humanity and work.

> "Work is the fundamental dimension of man's existence on earth, the proper subject of work continues to be man, and the finality of work is always man himself. There is no doubt that human work has an ethical value of its own, which clearly and directly remains linked to the fact that the one who carries it out is a person. Work is good for man – a good thing for his humanity – because through work man not only transforms nature, but he also achieves fulfillment as a human being and indeed, in a sense becomes 'more a human being'" (Laborem Exercens, Sept 1981).

Australian Catholics have forgotten significant parts of this message, if we are not a church centrally concerned with the dignity of work, in some real way we have forgotten the centrality of the human person and the centrality of our mission to mankind.

There are a number of veracious and moral dimensions to work we must rediscover. Firstly, there is no such thing as dead-end or worthless work. All work provides dignity, skills and financial independence. Low paid work is not demeaning to individuals, it actually performs an essential function as the first rung on the building of a career. 64% of low paid Australian workers move to higher wages within two years. This is contrary to what many Catholic organisations have been led to believe or promote themselves, nevertheless, low paid work is the beginning of income mobility.

After five years of work, only 3% of workers remain in low paid work and 75% have moved to higher paid work. (Submission to the fair work commission, annual wage review July 2019 – Institute of Public Affairs).

Low paid work equips workers with important experience, demonstrates reliability and a willingness to work, increases contacts and networks and teaches the standards of presentation and behaviour needed for successful, long term work.

The Catholic church has a fundamental interest in ensuring that these skills and habits are obtained. How can we seriously claim to be pro-humanity when we ignore this dimension and how can we seriously claim to be interested in marriage, family, the purchase of a house or sending of children to Catholic schools when we ignore the first rung of these "Catholic goods" – getting a job!

Nevertheless, the Australian commercial environment undermines workers, especially those looking for their first job in significant ways.

Our system imposes the highest minimum wage restrictions in the OECD. These high minimum wage requirements are a nefarious barrier and restriction to young Australians getting their first job. The Catholic church is completely silent on this issue. Our silence is unsatisfactory, particularly given our claims to uphold work as a central component on what it means to be human, indeed a dimension of human life that God has intended for our welfare.

For Catholics not to be advocating and leading in the provision of work, undermines Catholic claims to be co-creators with God and results in social outcomes, such as depression, drug use and disengagement with society. These outcomes are in fundamental opposition to our "calling" to transform the world and to draw all people to Christ.

There is no doubt that young Australians are suffering under our current system. 38% of 15-19 years old are underutilised in our workforce and a further 20% of 20-24 years old experience high levels of underutilisation. This means simply that young Australians are desiring more work and prepared to undertake increased hours of employment, yet our high minimum wages restrict employers from offering longer hours. The increasing Australian tend towards "casual" work is a direct outcome of this system. It seriously hurts young Australians, causes disengagement and depression and stifles the building of the "Catholic goals" of marriage, home, family and security. Yet, we continue in our silence!

The 2016 Australian census estimates that 250,000 Australians aged 15-24 are not engaged in any work nor undertaking any form of study. This cohort of young Australians already forms the basis of a significant "lost generation" that will potentially form an under-educated and disengaged community, carried into the future for many years.

The Catholic community has a significant moral challenge particularly if we continue to be complicit in blocking entry level and low paid work. We should be an organisation, above all others, that lower barriers to work and encourages young Australians to gain experience and improve their skills in the working environment.

What to do

So, what can the Catholic church do to be constructive in building employment and why is this a mission activity?

Firstly, we already have some successful examples. I have been fortunate to have been engaged in the provision of pre-employment programs for young Australians since 2013. These are voluntary programs, teaching young people the presentation, networking and personal skills necessary for employment. All of these 18-22 years old volunteer their time, have never worked previously, gain confidence and a deeper understanding of what work looks like. The "Mission Engage" program is conducted in business premises and uses mentors from these workplaces. All those who participate must dress for work. The unsurprising reality of that this enhances confidence and shows young people a clear and precise path to employment. What is stopping any diocese from such activities?

(www.missionengageyouth.org)

Additionally, all parishes/schools have a constant

need for maintenance, repair and gardening within their grounds. Why are we not undertaking the provision of entry level work to young, local and under-utilised Australians? Yes, there will be compliance, insurance and work safety issues – these are not insurmountable. The core problem is our lack of willingness to undertake such initiatives. If we only think in terms of "too hard baskets" we can hardly complain, we are unable to make a difference and that young Australians have no contact with the church nor are interested in it.

This is mission work at its most fundamental, it allows for the nurture of young Australians, it introduces them to local Catholics, it develops relationships, it harnesses parish energies and it makes lifelong connections. Does this make new "Catholics"? – ultimately this is Gods undertaking but if the Australian church does not prepare the soil, we are definitely not undertaking our part in showing Christian life in action to others.

(II) SUPPORT THE DISADVANTAGED AND BURDENED

Why

The foundation and starting point of Catholicism's perspective and approach to the disadvantaged and burdened is found in one of the great statements of Jesus, at the beginning of his public ministry. This mission statement establishes a strong correlation between who we are as his followers through to the kind of actions we should be taking.

> "And he opened the book and he found the place where it is written, the spirit of the Lord is upon me, because he has anointed me to proclaim the gospel to the poor, he has sent me to heal the broken-hearted, to proclaim deliverance to the captives and recovery of sight to the blind, to set at liberty those that are bruised. And he closed the book and gave it to the attendant, sat down and said, 'Today, this scripture is fulfilled in your hearing'" (Luke 4, 16-21).

Nevertheless, in recent decades I believe the church has misread the practical application of Christ's teachings and has disconnected mission and responsibility away from the fundamental purpose of creating a new society in which all people are to become active participates in the life of society and to contribute to the common good. The creation or maintenance of non-functioning individuals is not mission, nor is it helping the poor or building society. The activities of many Catholic aid agencies do not result in the changing of individual lives or of a changed society. Sadly, we are often contributing to an ongoing malaise made worse by its complete inability to illicit change.

There can be no doubt that Christ intended change to be part of his life and actions and also of his church. There is to be healing of the broken-hearted, deliverance for the captives, recovery of sight to the blind and liberty to the bruised. There is no mention here of failure, or of a model which leads people in the midst of chaos or hopelessness. The Catholic life is one of entry into new life and new ways of being, external life for Christ begins in our midst and is part of the transformation of our current lives.

Perhaps, an example of what not to do can be seen in the actions and attitude of one particular Melbourne parish. This parish has been engaged in the provision of free lunch time meals to around forty men, all in their late 30's and early 40's. These men were what the long serving parish priest described as "survivors of the 1980's drug wars".

I encountered these men in around 2010, where the lunch had been in operation for nearly 30 years. The same men continued to attend, nothing was asked of them, despite an overgrown garden, no work was suggested. When asked why nothing was expected from them, it was stated that they were all hopeless, they had suffered and weren't expected to change or develop in any way. My experience of these men suggested much could have been required and many could have been integrated substantially into community life. They were not hopeless nor intellectually incapable.

The form of Catholic "service" offered to them was essentially valueless, it changed nothing and whilst it kept them physically alive it offered nothing in the way of Catholic new life or a future back into society. This is not mission; it is a feel-good exercise for those who provide the service.

The Catholic church has in a number of welfare organisations taken to using the phrase "a preferential option for the poor" this phrase is never unpacked in meaning other than to suggest Jesus was concerned for the economically poor.

Nevertheless, poverty has a much deeper perspective in Catholic thinking, for Christ, perhaps the poorest people were those, who despite personal wealth had no idea how far away they were from God's Kingdom. If we just see poverty in exclusively economic terms and accept that poor people can't change, then in what ways are we actually bringing about the Kingdom of God? Christ's preferential option was actually a challenge to all of us, to make changes in our lives, to become active participates in the "body of Christ", the emphasis here is one of contribution leading to change of society. It is not hopeless; it demands change and it is set within a format of "making disciples of all nations". It is very valuable work to keep individuals fed and warm and alive, but without change it is not what Jesus called his followers to do.

In most modern Western nations who are generally wealthy a new and insidious type of poverty has arisen. Unfortunately, again it is a poverty that Catholicism seems in practical ways to be ignoring or not engaged against.

Recently, the United States and Iceland both announced that they had eradicated "Downs Syndrome". The Australian medical profession has welcomed this outcome. Of course, they have not discovered a cure for down's syndrome, what they have is an early blood test that indicates at around eight weeks if an unborn child carries the genetic fault. The parents are then pressured to abort this child, after having been bombarded with information regarding the difficulties of raising such children.

Poverty in many western societies has little to do with economics, but as in this case, a serious loss of respect for the vulnerable, the intellectually challenged or those with other birth deformities. On our path to a perfect world we are finding less room for those who do not fit our "designer future" visions of humanity.

During the 1930's and 1940's, the Catholic church was the major opponent of the Nazi action T4, involuntary euthanasia programme, under which the mentally ill physically deformed and incurably sick were killed. The euthanasia program began in 1939 and ultimately resulted in the murder of around 70,000 individuals which included the senile, mentally ill and children with Down Syndrome. The Catholic bishop Clemens August von Galen who led the opposition was able to close the program in combination with widespread public opposition.

Is it in 2020 a reasonable question to ask if our modern western world is manifestly different from the Germany of the Nazi era? What is noticeable is the church failure to garnish enough support and attention to these growing practices. Supporting the disadvantaged and burdened in modern Australia is no longer exclusively an enterprise centring on economic poverty. The poverty of modern Australia is often concealed and inconspicuous in our futuristic desire for a perfect and meticulous world. The work of organisations like Downs Syndrome Australia, Deaf-Blind Australia, Brain Injury Australia and Asperger's Australia and the many families with special needs children in our parish midst need our support, along with those who boldly see a different vision for Australia's future.

Be Local: Down Syndrome Example

There may be some advocacy advisory networks and local families engaged in the long-term battle of changing attitudes and increasing educational opportunities, employment and health outcomes. Pre-natal support and support for parents with a Downs Syndrome child is valuable work.

Again, connecting to a local family and discussing ways to make local connections, add a great deal to not only the family concerned but to their wider local connections as well.

Family to family contacts allow a greater assessment of what the family needs might be, along with what they can do for you.

Authentic Mission is not a one-way street and few parishes have the necessary skills to make a short-term difference. Trust is the important factor to develop but families with a down syndrome child are not beggars.

In the first instance establish some dialogue between parish families and your possible connections. A wide family to family network will also bring much to the families that already attend your parish.

Family life is difficult for all families so it won't just be a family with a disability that might need support making connections. Considering ways that all families in your region may develop and could produce some interesting initiatives that improve the attractiveness of your community life. It is not necessary for a parish to have an obvious set of objectives for commencing mission but a joining together in discussion with others within your parish boundaries may bring forth some mutually beneficial ideas and initiatives.

What to Do

Adopt a Family

Establishing family to family contacts is an important first step. Primarily this requires a network of interested families from the parish side, who are familiar with their own difficulties and can see some opportunities of mutual benefit with a family that has a Down's Syndrome child. Enabling some discussion opportunities between families will be essential as trust needs to develop and the first point of call shouldn't be the parish priest. Certainly, the priest can be a guide and a mentor but connectedness runs better when the families are able to establish their own connections and come up with their own beneficial initiatives. Such a methodology is likely to also ensure that any joint mission activities have the embrace of all families involved. Allowing mission sub-groups of families to evolve is a powerful way to undertake local mission and also to come up with ideas that would never have been considered by those not experiencing the day to day struggle of the Australian family.

Create a Job Network

Employment is a key component of independence for people with Down's Syndrome. Finding pathways to secure employment and employers who don't exploit individuals with Downs Syndrome is not always easy. In many areas disability employment services are able to contribute some funds towards helping people maintain a job.

Nevertheless, the important considerations rest with the parish for those considering taking on a Down's Syndrome worker. Establishing an environment of trust and security is important, expectations will need modification and a strong match between an individual's abilities and interests and parish needs would need to be found. There are always obstacles in matching any Australian to a new job, yet the potential for growth, improvement in lifestyle and the establishment of new friends is profound for those prepared to give disabled individuals a chance. Parishes do have a large amount of part time work that could be created and tailored to a worker with Down's Syndrome. Often there are significant opportunities for the provision of such work, if will power and patience can be added to the mix, powerful connections are possible.

Social Groups

People with Down's Syndrome are often involved in a wide range of community activities. Nevertheless, there are significant barriers which, unfortunately, can include discrimination and community hostility. There is no reason for this to be experienced within the parish context and there is a great deal that parishes could offer. Fitness groups, dance classes, martial arts groups, coffee mornings. There is no reason why people with Down Syndrome should also not participate in the liturgical life of a parish. Naturally, care should be taken to ensure inclusion is not just a token action but the involvement of Down Syndrome people brings more to your parish than perhaps you may initially realise.

Affordable Housing

It may be the case that in some parish communities' opportunities to convert buildings are available. Individuals with Down Syndrome usually do not have significant funds yet reaching the point of independent living is the ultimate step in making individual life choices and growing into a fully functioning human being. Within the Australian context there is a huge disadvantage in connecting people with Down Syndrome to a life where choice increases, new friends can be made and a strong contribution to Australian society is possible. The Catholic parish could play a vital role is developing a more equitable place for Down Syndrome Australians.

Education

In many environments the local Catholic parish school is struggling. Numbers can be low and in toughened economic circumstances many parents delay funding for Catholic education to the secondary years. Nevertheless, the beauty of Catholic life is often found in the personalised and community nature of these schools. Families, teachers and students can develop lifelong connections from the sense of security and nature these schools develop. They are also the perfect environment for a family with a Down Syndrome child.

These smaller numbers encourage the possibility of an easier and less overwhelming connectedness. It may be possible for local parishes to offer a family with a Down Syndrome child a placement within a Catholic parish school.

Connecting your parish community with the Australian Down Syndrome community is important work. Increasingly, this community is finding itself under stress and facing substantial hidden discrimination. Families of whatever background who make a decision for life deserve our support.

(III) HELP SINGLE PARENTS

Why?

Single parent families in Australia appear to have reached a state of statistical equilibrium, yet this situation continues to remain decidedly averse to individuals within single parent families.

Single parent families make up around 14% of all families with 82% of these being led by women. This figure is unchanged over the last twenty odd years and its predicted to be unchanged into the 2040's. From a Catholic perspective, perhaps a developing concern is the number of families without children which is currently sitting at 38%. This leaves the largest group of families as couples with children, making up 43% of families.

Catholicism as a faith is centrally concerned with the safety and development of children within a family incorporating, male and female parents, but we need to accept reality and focus on the important dimension of supporting children in families, whatever type of family that is. The statistical increase of families without children is also a concern for Catholicism, but a more immediate concern, often seen but not acted upon is the support needed by single mothers and fathers.

Statistics from the United States, which have not been surveyed in the Australian context, point to a wider concern with families happy to label themselves as Catholic. Only 66% of those families say that first communion is important and only 61% see confirmation as relevant for their children.

Plainly Catholic families are becoming less connected to the sacramental life. There is no statistical information to suggest that a flimsy adherence to the sacramental life leads to a feeble adult expression of Catholicism, yet the smallish numbers of 18-35 year olds found in Australian Catholic churches would suggest this is the reality. Catholics must stop talking about the importance of family and start acting this truth in our community life.

Paradoxically, such a focus of Christian life also brings another positive by-product for Catholic communities, it reconnects us to the great concern of all Australians (not climate change or refugee intakes) but will our children have meaningful work in the future? And will this work provide a quality of life that will allow then to marry, to have families, to own a house and to educate their own children and grandchildren?

These "Catholic goods" are all under significant stress in modern Australia, unfortunately the group of Australians who should be speaking out loudly about our community life, the Catholic church is completely silent on such vital and core difficulties. A Catholic parish community which adopts initiatives for young unemployed, or those who have lost jobs later in life, unveils a bold statement about the future direction for our country. Seeking to be a focal point in the vital question of work, places Catholics at the centre of the great concern for our community. Remaining actionless and silent will continue to see the church on the periphery of Australian life.

Be Local

Unemployment, particularly youth unemployment is widespread in almost all Australian communities, city, rural and on urban fringes. An opening opportunity is usually available for the commencement of young people's work in and around parish buildings or in a network of parishioners that need local tasks performed. Some research through local government and local council statistics will often indicate levels of unemployment, statistics in relation to those studying, the level and types of work that often go on in your area, but most importantly, what is missing in your area? What work functions are absent? And what are the numbers of those who fail to participate in any way? This information will give you an overview that may allow for some creative and exciting local initiatives, based out of your community. Who you choose to involve, why you're doing your initiative and those who benefit from the initiative, are at the centre of mission. Young people from single parent backgrounds often lack mentors and local networks that could be provided by motivated parishioners

What to Try

Teach some work skills

Most parishes contain a significant residual of work skills both in parishioners still working or in those recently retired. In most areas of Australia, unemployment agencies no longer operate practical training programs they administer courses through on-line learning.

There is a significant discrepancy between on-line comprehension and the hands-on training that can be delivered by motivated and enthusiastic mentors. Having a person with significant business and workplace knowledge grants to young unemployed Australians a level of discernment and proficiency, no online program can offer. This dimension of presentation, interview techniques, public speaking, body language, CV development and just the acquisition of confidence is a huge advantage to an individual who has never been through an interview process or successfully obtained a job. There is a significant gap in the preparation of young Australians for work, that could be fulfilled by smart and driven Catholic communities.

Connect your parish with mission-engage youth

Undoubtably, mission-engage youth has transformed the methodology and approach to gaining young Australians their first job. The program works in the opposite manner to all other pre-employment channels. At mission-engage young Australians are taken into workplaces to meet workers, to see what business and companies actually do, the hours worked, the dress codes, the kind of jobs available, the process for gaining work and clear visions for the changes young people might have to make. This process shows young people what work is actually like and what is needed to gain and hold a job.

It is not about what a young person thinks work is like, but the actual requirements to get there and the confidence to do so. The transformation in young people is usually profound, working becomes vitally seen as achievable, (perhaps for the first time) connections and networks are built and mentor relationships can be developed and maintained. There is no reason why the mentoring, coaching and nurturing of young unemployed people cannot be conducted or channelled through the local parish. Working, mentoring and developing local networks is the key to getting and holding a first job.

The value that young Australians receive, their gratefulness and their ongoing desire to maintain connections to where they live is an outstanding contribution that parish communities can make to both their own young people and to their wider community. The power of this connection should not be underestimated. How many current Australian Catholic parishes play such a vital and ongoing role in their local communities today? (www.missionengageyouth.org).

Offer Local Part-Time Work around the Parish

Most parishes have a great deal of part-time work, maintenance projects and gardening upkeep. Why not consider employing a young Australian who has little history of work, to undertake parish upkeep under the supervision of a retired parishioner or other qualified locals prepared to help. Initial outlays will include work overalls, proper shoes and safety vests, along with an introductory salary. The easiest commencement jobs might include painting, gardening or some minor administration. Insurance implications will be present but don't be put off by these small hurdles. The impact on a young local is powerful and long-lasting. Getting your parish known as a community that works in life changing ways with young people is a striking message to your local community. The cost of such a program could be funded by one parish collection per week, the difference in this case, is that the money stays local and the persuasive message resides with your local parish, unlike most collections for social welfare which vanish into central funds without neighbourhood results.

I have personally been involved in many such programs, the results and long-term changes to individual lives can be profound. Disasters and failures will also abound, yet the successful completion of 8-10 weeks of work is a first-rate outcome for a local parish community. Such progress draws young people to your community and indicates to those who live within your boundaries, the seriousness of your faith!

In some instances, government money may be available but often comes with strings attached. Starting small and undertaking a thorough selection program can raise the chances of success and often sees a longer-term young person's connection to your community life.

Develop a Not for Profit Local Op-Shop on your Premises

Opportunity shops can be sustained for comparatively low cost, particularly if parish premises can be used to remove rent and a parish is prepared to bear utility costs. The provision of goods will largely come through parishioners and their connections. The profit from this enterprise can be used for an income to those who work within the shop. This initiative provides an excellent grounding for understanding the retail sector, handling finances, arranging stock, pricing and customer service. This is a particularly good grounding for young people with little experience in interpersonal relationships and in the processes of organising multiple tasks.

Sponsor an Internship

Entry Level work is a diminishing sector in the Australian workplace, increasingly high-end companies are looking for already qualified workers, therefore there are significant opportunities for local communities to be involved in the provision of entry level work.

Opportunities also exist where a parish might consider "paying" for a short-term internship at a local business, the parish would be responsible for the attendance, presentation, understanding workplace requirements and general work ethic. In many instances, this kind of "internship" transforms into full time work, given that the workplace has seen a motivated and determined to learn young person. Many workplaces are prepared to bare future costs for the right person. In this instance the "internship" becomes a long job interview, allows workplaces to fully assess character and willingness to learn and from a parish perspective you have acted on making your community more viable and yourselves more recognisable as a "mission" community.

Connections with Local Schools

There are always a smallish number of students who have a firm grasp of their future and have chosen their future university and field of study. The majority are not in this position, many are demotivated in school, and may not yet have found a passion or long-term work interest. There are also significant numbers who find school difficult and are keen to begin a working life but find themselves "underdone" in skills or preparation for a transaction to work.

Developing a solid relationship with local Catholic and secondary schools often provide a good number of young people and families to interview and help prepare for work. These relationships take time to develop but if you are able to offer training, some skills, or a short-term internship the rewards and transformations are profound. It is often an unusual position for a parish to be so valued by a local family and to have made such a difference to a young son or daughter. The impact of such interventions is long lasting and often not forgotten locally. Australian Catholics need these kinds of "mission interventions" that change lives. We currently make little local difference by exclusively sending our mission envelopes to diocese for work usually not seen or heard of again. In my view, it's time for a change.

(IV) BATTING FOR AUSTRALIA

Why

The compelling and overwhelming fact is that Australia Day is extensively supported by the vast majority of Australians. The 2020 poll conducted by Dynata found that only 11% of Australians think the date should be changed, whilst 85% were proud to be Australians, only 5% were found to disagree. Australia is a great place to live, build a new life and start a family. Australians are fundamentally optimistic and positive about Australia and its values.

Unfortunately, Australia Day is another sphere where Catholicism is largely silent, it rarely makes statements of pride in our societal culture, nor indeed our Catholic culture, which has given so much to the wider community. The disconnection between Catholics and the wider community is not helped by the silence of Catholic leaders, nor the reluctance to celebrate the many achievements of our nation. We are truly a unique democracy, culture and nation of new beginnings and achievement. Why can't Catholic bishops celebrate and highlight this achievement?

The 2020 Dynata poll also found that 71% of Australians believe Australia has a history to be proud of, only 13% thought otherwise, 70% thought that there should be less political disagreement over Australia Day – only 11% disagreed. 71% believe

Australia day is an authentic way for indigenous and non-indigenous Australians, to celebrate being Australian, only 12% disagreed.

83% of Australians thought Australia day should be an opportunity to respect the contribution that everyone has and can make to Australia. Wouldn't these sentiments be a wonderful voice of unity coming from the bishops of the Catholic church!

Australians are tired of the negative narrative that tells us to be ashamed of our history and culture rather than celebrating our achievements. The 26th of January marks the foundation of modern Australia and the freedoms that are enjoyed by all Australians. What a difference it would make if the Catholic bishops could joyously celebrate our community life, not denigrate its achievements through underwhelming praise or silence.

On some occasions disaffected people would have us believe that patriotism is incompatible or in competition with Catholicism. Yet love of country, the nation that nurtured us goes hand in hand with other Catholic virtues of love of family and duty to neighbours. We receive the faith locally, we live it in our families, we utter it in our own tongues, we practice it in a building with people from this community. In this way Australia has nurtured our faith. Patriotism is not to be confused with notions of superiority or a view that pursues the advantages of your country at the expense of others.

The authentic Australian loves his nation, in the same way he loves his parents, his family, his local institutes and its unique sports. These are the things that have nurtured and framed his life. Catholic culture is called to love Australian culture and in doing so transforms its heart. This is the Australia all Catholics are called to strengthen and uphold. God calls us to make disciples of all nations and that includes Australia.

Be Local

The vast majority of local councils, community clubs and sporting clubs hold some form of local Australia day celebrating our community life. Why not our parishes? Some groups offer Breakfast, food stalls, children and family entertainment along with citizenship awards and ceremonies. It may be possible to join with another community group or offer a stand-alone activity displaying Catholic ways of life to your wider community. Catholicism is called by Christ to change the world; it begins by having the courage to proudly proclaim our culture.

What to Do

Host a BBQ

At some stage, perhaps either side of Australia day, your parish could host an Australia day BBQ, with community events, invite other groups, provide children activities or host an Australia day Ambassador to speak at your event.

Hosting testimonies from those who have endured significant hardship to come to Australia is a powerful and effective way of bonding to others but also of making plain how lucky we are and the benefits Australians all enjoy.

We do have a tendency to imagine that all will be well in Australia, yet Catholicism is under suspicion and scrutiny as perhaps never before in our history. We have a strong viewpoint on the direction of Australia life, but we hardly every articulate this sufficiently or demonstrate our culture to the wider community. Persecution arises when communities become disconnected from those around them and our purpose of transformation can hardly take place if we remain disconnected and unseen. Hosting our fellow Australians on our property is a useful first step.

Become Ambassadors

Joining in the process of creating parishioners to be local ambassadors is another step-in promoting Catholicism and our powerful view in what sort of nation we should be. Other cultures are quite happy to connect Australia to the values they uphold. Why should Catholics be so reticent? Our story is a great story within the wider community, yet we appear self-conscious in its promotion. We have much to be proud of in Australia, indeed it is our culture that is a foundational one in relation to education, hospitals, hospices and care of the elderly.

As it stands in 2020, we are unfortunately failing to lead, particularly in relation to marriage and family stress, unemployment, youth issues and drug abuse. Catholicism is an essential dimension to Australian life, it is time, we proudly proclaimed it again. Australia day is an opportunity to bring something important to the table. We don't come empty handed when we highlight Catholicism.

Fly the Flag

Very few of our parishes or schools fly the Australian flag on our buildings. We do fly a great deal of other flags usually ones belonging to particular groups. We should be less confused about the focus, love and central position that Australia holds for us. It is to our nation that we are called to direct our transformational goals, not specific groups, returning to the central task in an important aspect of Australia day.

Run an Australia Day Initiative in your School

The connection between Australia and Catholicism is rarely made in our schools. Most of our schools are concerned with social justice issues not with understanding how Australia has been substantially formed by Catholicism.

An "Australia Day" within school time, highlighting our connections with the essence of our nation is a good way to build both pride in our nation and faith. Guest speakers (perhaps parents) who have fought to leave troubled nations and endured hardships to enjoy our freedom, speak strongly to the "Catholic values" of freedom, democracy, women's rights and free enterprise which underpin our national life. Student speakers who have arrived in Australia with little material wealth but a family Catholicism are a strong example of the connection of our faith and wider economic prosperity and safety. A nation that loses it strong "ethical values" will very quickly lose its material wealth as well. Our values underpin the Australian story, we should unashamedly make this case to young Australians.

Parish Partnerships

Not all Catholic parishes are economically viable, but all of them are central to the beauty of Catholicism within their various communities. We cannot afford to lose or close Catholic communities no matter how small they may be.

Australia day offers an opportunity for financially secure parishes to contribute to another that is "struggling". This should be on a parish to parish level, developing relationships, understanding each other's needs and vision and trying to make a difference to each other. This does not need to be a financial arrangement, but it should be about meeting, talking and holding some functions together.

We share the gift of Christ's life to us, we can always

learn from others. Australia day is a good opportunity to cement those joint relationships, people to people exchanges or fund-raising events. Travelling to each other or staying with local parishioners could also be an option. Jointly, operating an Authentic Mission idea is one or other or both of the parishes also has potential. In some circumstance's relationships with parishes from New Zealand or South East Asia may be comparatively affordable and viable. There are no rights or wrongs on this spectrum. All that is required is an openness to some new ideas. Australia day provides an excellent opportunity to share and understand our different expressions of Australia along with the uniqueness of our Catholic culture in your area.

Sponsor your own Australian of the Area Trophy

Sporting clubs have player recognition and trophy presentations every year. They also reward long serving individuals or those who have made outstanding commitments to the life of the club. Why don't parishes do the same? These recognitions are not only about the individual but are strong ways of building community and thanking people for their efforts. The Catholic church is usually very poor at such recognition, sometimes our besottedness with the role of the priest, blinds us to the fabulous and long-term work of others. Australia day offers significant opportunities to properly thank your own people and those involved in the life of the wider community that are not your parishioners. Thanking and rewarding people is a great way to build and sustain new partnerships.

Tree Planting activities on Australia Day

Tree planting ceremonies offer another visible and lasting methods of thanking and honouring those who contribute so much to your community life. This is not usually expensive but gives the opportunity to present a significant reward for those who have lived their Catholicism in your midst. It is also an excellent opportunity to invite family, friends and others to see how Catholics appreciate and honour their life together. The opportunities to highlight the Catholic life and culture to others in your wider community are manifold on Australia Day.

(V) GENERATION ADRIFT

Over the last twenty years, the Australian community has witnessed a dramatic rise in difficulties and problems associated with young Australians. In many ways there appears to be no resolution to the enigma currently affecting young Australians. They are a generation severely affected by depression, they have extensive issues in transitioning to work, often have no concept of what they hope for from life, are sometimes disconnected from parents and family, and many are enthralled to a life of illicit drug use.

A general malaise of de-motivation and inertia seems to have befallen large numbers of 18-22-year olds, which is now being transferred into the years beyond 25. This generation often has limited plans or expectations for marriage, family, home ownership or wider community commitments. Of course, this is not the experience for all of our young Australians, but numbers are now significant enough to draw generalised conclusions and understandings of future troubles for these individuals unless something can change soon.

Anecdotally, I would layer a number of broad generalisations to this mix of information. In large measure, the children of migrants seem largely unaffected, it appears very much a home-grown phenomenon and secondly the Catholic church is having absolutely no impact or influence over 18-22 year old Australians.

In recent years, some Catholic diocese have mistakenly sought to immerse themselves in digital technology as a method to help stop young people from leaving the church in significant numbers. This had not produced any results of lasting duration. It is important we move away from the gimmicks of apps, rock masses and dance performance.

In my view investing in "Catholic culture", work programs and giving young Australians responsibilities offers more long-term opportunities but this involves significant hard work; and a long-term commitment to re-connecting with young people across a number of life facets. The disconnection between Australian parishes and their local schools remains a serious obstruction to the task of mission in the Australian context.

The Absence of the Young from Mass

The truth of the Catholic experience for young Australians is not a pretty one. Disconnection leading to disaffiliation is an overwhelming normal experience in every Australian diocese. We are in crisis. An American study on young adults leaving the Catholic church found that many young people stopped identifying as Catholics on average at 13 years of age. When delving deeper into the study more than 50% said that although they identified as Catholics, they had attended mass on average only around twice a year. Whilst 2/3 had made their first communion less than a third had received confirmation and almost 60% had never received any instruction or belonged to a Catholic youth group.

I have no doubt our Australian circumstances are similar; we have minor success engaging with primary aged Catholics but have almost zero impact on the Catholic teenager or beyond. Unless we are prepared to specially target this age group and devote substantial resources, nothing will change.

Three Youth Components: One New Idea

Many Catholic parishes can identify 3 particular components to the youth in their parishes:

(i) The primary school aged child
(ii) The secondary aged young person, and
(iii) The 18-22-year-old, both those attending University and those not

The secular media and psychologists identify huge problems in each sector, but really have no answer to these problems. They are good at pointing out the problems but without any workable answers.

Catholic parishes need to be positive about each sector because we have distinctive answers that we know have worked, yet in the Australian context we have given up applying them. Let's think in more depth about each sector.

The Primary School

Most Catholic parishes have a primary school attached to their complex. Most of these small schools are disconnected from their parish base. Indeed, parishioners never go into the school and the school rarely attends mass, unless in preparation for first communion and confirmation. In truth, the two aspects of Catholic life are starkly separated.

Having been a former school Chaplain for 16 years, I know that in large measure these students are very faithful, they are keen to listen and keen to believe. Yet, too much of what we teach them is transitory and trivial. Unbelievably some of our primary school students are living on a diet of social justice, many are told of Australian and Catholic injustice to indigenous Australians (a very partial story!) some schools have been involved in organised demonstrations against government policy on Refugees or immigration or climate change. It is hardly surprising we have distressed and confused these very young Australians. This is not what the teaching of Catholicism needs to be about in the primary years. These early years must be about pride in the faith, the great story of what Catholicism has done for Australia, the heroic life of Jesus, and a large diet of the courage of saints who stood up against persecution and changed their societies. Such a curriculum is based on optimism and achievement, not shame or despair.

The Secondary School

The secondary school years often witness both the beginning of Catholic rejection and its total abandonment by year 11 and 12. It is extremely difficult for parishes to keep connections with their secondary school aged young people. These young Australians are either dependant on family to bring them to mass or are more likely to have developed all sorts of reasons for not attending with the family. In some ways teenage separation from the family is normal and we need to accept the fact that mass is often viewed as long, boring or repetitive.

The only way of keeping these young teenagers is to offer things that are not seen as embarrassing and a place when they can be with friends. This means specific initiatives that allows their engagement and contribution and encourages them to share such initiatives with their friends. This makes youth work missionary! Some areas of focus might be dance classes, martial arts groups, outdoor activities, cooking or a host of other specific skilled activities.

These are usually possible for parishes to conduct but you must make them as cheap as possible. Many young Australians want to do these activities but they have little money and family budgets may prevent them. There is a significant gap that parishes can fill, particularly if the majority of your young people do not attend fee paying private schools or cannot afford commercial alternatives in your neighbourhood. It's your job to bring a subtle Catholic component to these initiatives, they are not to be secular but primarily should provide another layer of "Catholic vibe" without turning people away.

18-22-year old

This grouping seems to be the most impacted by mental health, lack of confidence and depression. Having experienced an Australian school system that talks incessantly about opportunities and developing the individual into an unlimited creative being, it is not hard to envisage a period of instability when confronting the real world for the first time.

Jobs are hard to come by, and the reality for many Australians will be a working environment that requires the layering of 2-3 jobs at any one time. Lifetime jobs are increasingly hard to find, and all work now requires constant retraining and adaption. It is one of the ironies of the Australian education system that despite much talk of unlimited opportunities, little has been undertaken to allow young Australians to make regular change and adapt to a new and unpredictable world.

This in my view, is at the heart of much of Australia's under 24 mental health issues. Life is a wonderful and exciting adventure, but it requires constant change and adaption, the abandonment of many dreams and the ability to layer different dimensions into one life.

Additionally, we no longer talk about vocation, that is the feeling of a unique calling, which in the catholic framework is a calling from God to do something specific for him. Why do we no longer talk about vocation in our schools and parishes. I have met many people empowered and energised by a sense of vocation, what I can guarantee that is that none of these people were depressed, self-harming or contemplating suicide. The urgency of a vocation drove them to continually seek to fulfill these tasks in new and unique ways with as many people as possible. This in essence is the Catholic life in action.

Vocation is a far deeper phenomenon than positive thinking or attitudes, it cannot be worked up by positive self-talk or thinking but at its foundation it is the very heart of who this person is. That is the gift, Jesus promises to us in new life, we need again to be talking and highlighting vocation in our Catholic parishes and schools.

Vocation is more than an antidote for mental health issues as it drives life itself, its bi-product is purposeful energised and vibrant human beings. For our 18-22 years old we should be focused not on the world of unlimited possibilities or experiences but on the wonder of a unique purpose and manifestation of a vocation: What are you going to do in life that makes a difference to others? And how can your parish enable this to happen in our midst? Catholicism is not a club; it is a life lived in service and commitment to Christ and to others.

Pope John Paul II often spoke about the culture

of death. This culture is all around us, not that we are surrounded by mass murders, but that we are surrounded by many people who are enamoured by nothing. Life consists of a series of experiences, a little overseas travel for a young Australian, a succession of work without passion, a family life disconnected from children and an overarching feeling that there must be more.

This is not a bad life, but a life without vocation and therefore subjected to constant change without satisfaction. We cannot have more of the same, over and over, and continue to believe that our lives are making a difference. Here is the heart of vocation and Catholic life: making a difference for others actually makes a difference to us!

It is often noted that migrant communities and their children make a powerful difference to our wider community and to themselves. This is usually due to an unspoken recognition that life is urgent: when you come to a new country, without many resources, you are busy forming your life, busy working, busy taking on more than you can usually cope with, life is a constant question of what can I do next, what can my children do? What will my family do? This urgency is born of knowing what doing nothing or not having a job means in their former country, hunger and possible death! In the migrant community, urgency often leads to continuous forms of employment and ultimately success.

This is not to suggest the migrant experience is a perfect model, but its parallel and more positive adaptation is a vocation that brings us to a similar consideration: what can I do next? How can I make a difference? What does God call me to do in these circumstances? This set of questions and style of thinking has largely disappeared from the Australian community. Here, I believe Catholicism has another opportunity to make a difference to our parishes, school and wider communities. Each of our parishes and schools must become powerhouses for vocation and the life of making a difference. Do this and the bi-product of healthier young Australians will ensure.

Be Local

In many instances, a parish has a connection to a local small Catholic school. It is important to make an honest assessment of your relationship with your school, the reality of your connectedness and if this is lacking commence an effort of improvement.

It is also of value that it is not only the priest who is connecting to the school, other parishioners, suitably disposed and interested in the school must also be involved in encounters with Headmasters and staff. The parish must also be prepared to initiate some local initiatives to improve the relationship. Don't come to your school community empty handed! You challenge them to engage with you, through them seeing you as people of ideas and innovation. This is a process of each part of the local Catholic expression seeing each other as a valuable resource. There is no problem if your suggested initiatives are not taken up, be prepared to demand in return some ideas from their end for strengthening and improving the relationship.

What to Do

The Primary School

In the first instance, the parish might develop a small group of vibrant parishioners prepared to visit the school as a team. The idea is to talk about the parish, tell personal stories of why you are there. Share positive things about the work you do in the parish and your life together. Be prepared with your priest to ensure that some jobs will be available for young students to do. Altar serving is a particular easy win, but training and parents' permission will be needed. More than one parishioner is needed to encourage and highlight this role. With thought there are many other jobs/roles students can undertake. Consider students for singing/reading and helping with various pre-mass jobs. This will certainly be an initial burden, yet the greater goal of getting your students seeing the mass as a positive outweighs the inconvenience.

Class Masses at the Parish

At least once a month, a class mass should be operating via one of the grades in your school. This means all of the preparation, readings, crucifers, acolytes, servers and those bringing up the gifts are all from the grade: Parents are required but an important sub message might be delivered; send your children to Catholic school and actually risk they might become Catholic! If this model proves difficult in your environment, move the mass and a small clutch of parishioners into the school hall for a similar grade mass. The more you do this the more normal it becomes!

Parishioners involvement in the R.E. Program

Religious instruction is a central subject in a Catholic school. Nevertheless, it can be a subject that is often presented in an Ad Hoc way across many of our schools. This is not a reflection on individual teachers but within a busy curriculum it can be occasionally viewed as less central than it actually is. It may well be that RE teachers would welcome greater input from members of the parish community, particularly in sharing personal stories and lives of the saints, two areas very neglected in Catholic schools.

The possibilities for greater involvement from the parish is endless, yet forming a dedicated and motivated group of parishioners may be a longer-term difficulty. The parish community is often disappointed in the level of attendance at mass from their local school, yet the lack of connected and personal relationships is often a barrier. A parish prepared to undertake the "risk" of greater engagement in their school (not only through the priest) is usually rewarded with a greater working relationship with its school.

Engaging the School Music Program in Parish Life

A strong relationship with the school music co-ordinator, could see a regular component of parish mass, be provided through class singing including choirs, duets or soloists. Possibilities are endless but hard work and relationships are required.

Youth Groups and Specialist Activities

Parishes might consider the appointment of a youth worker to begin the creation of youth activities in the parish. This is a difficult role, hard to sustain for the individual concerned and usually involving slow starts and small numbers. Nevertheless, with the right person great things are possible. The youth worker should be imbedded for some small hours within the local school. This aids credibility and allows the youth worker to be seen and heard over longer periods of time. Youth workers that are only parish based have a much higher percentage of failure, not because of the individuals concerned, but due to the smaller amount of exposure with young people. The appointment of a parish youth worker should involve some access to the school community, teachers and parents.

Secondary School

Most parishes do not have access to secondary school in similar manner to the primary school.

Nevertheless, there are a large number of initiatives that can be considered by a parish or youth worker hoping to work with secondary aged children. If such a school sits within your parish boundaries, it will certainly be worth talking to the headmaster in charge of the school. This is a much harder environment given the obvious lack of connection with the parish; however, a few things could be considered.

Youth Mentoring within the School

Many students lack trusted adult mentors in school, this model has had some success being offered exclusively by secular organisations. In school mentoring opportunities (ISMO) are offered by a number of organisations, the model is not a difficult one to duplicate. Most of these initiatives are complementary to the school welfare program. Mentors are required to undertake short training courses and secure working with children and police checks. It may be possible for parishes to form small teams of mentors that can be offered to students who could do with some additional support and inspiration.

Vocational Talks to Students

It may be possible for your parish to form a small group of parishioners focused specially on the question of vocation: What is it? How to discover it? Why it is important? And how it helps others and you? This can be particularly valuable to a parish if you have your own mission programs that you would like young Australians to join or if you are able to engage the school in something that needs doing within the local area. Projects with a human and environmental focus seem to resonate with many teenager students. Working with secondary schools will always involve, creating some enthusiasm in an initiative that you bring to the school. Importantly, it should be your program, with your parishioners involved, without this, credibility and longevity are difficult to sustain. Initiatives might involve, the creation of gardens, animal refuge or welfare initiatives to local residents. Some research will be required on the needs of the local environment and on the interests of the school community.

Specific Youth Activities

Very few secondary schools are able to offer courses catering to the interests of all students. Huge gaps between student interests and school offerings usually exist. Some research will enable motivated parishioners to discover what these might be. For example, not all schools will have, after school, cooking and dance classes, theatre groups, dog training, painting classes or out of school tuition. The list of such possibilities is endless. Importantly, these initiatives should be conducted with school approval but on your parish premises, with your parishioners involved. That's the point, it's about drawing young Australians into your community, to see and experience you as both a safe and useful community. Such initiatives take patience and persistence but are worth the long-term efforts. No Catholic parish in Australia is a natural haven for 13-18-year old's yet some initiatives can work, parishes need to make the initial effort and the initial contacts.

Employment Expos

Hosting employment expos may be an excellent way of getting your parish known in the wider community. It makes sense to conduct these after consultation with local schools to understand a little more of what their needs and requirements might be. Nevertheless, schools are notoriously poor at understanding the world of work and better partners will naturally be local companies or workforces themselves.

If you are a parish with a large employer in your area, partner with them, even if they have no work available, they will usually see these as useful public relations opportunities. A large local Bunnings, Coles, Woolworths, local banks and other retails may be happy to provide staff to explain jobs, roles, training, salary and qualifications and future opportunities. These are the essential things that parents, and students wish to know but are not always available at most expos. If you have the ability within the parish to offer support in creating CV's, job interview techniques or public speaking be prepared to advertise the kind of things that you are able to contribute. Initially, these may not be seen as areas of natural Catholic expertise. This is because we have been out of this field for many decades, nevertheless, the provision of and advocacy for work is Catholic Social Justice, 101. A parish prepared to move back into this field will gain enormous credibility as this is the great concern for average Australians, how to get and hold employment and the development of jobs that can bring lifelong work satisfaction.

18-22 Years Old

Preparing for the world of work is a huge issue for 18-22-years-old Australians. Overwhelmingly, schools have not prepared students for the realities of work, for dress codes, personal appearance, turning up on time and not disparaging your company on social media. For many young Australians the material on Facebook posted under their name may have a significant detrimental impact on future work prospects. Students need to be aware of this and be coached on how to post, positive and enlightened messages about themselves and the things they support and believe in. The numbers of young Australians barred from work by imagining that such mediums are private is extremely high.

I would strongly support partnering with mission engage youth, to look at hosting a training course in your parish, that seeks to show 18-22-year olds what work is actually like. This program works by bringing young people into various workplaces, meeting those who actually work in the businesses and seeing how particular jobs actually function. This reality check helps young people to modify their understandings of work and to prepare more fully for moving into a job. It also provides greater clarity on the levels of passion needed to grow and hold work. There is a huge gap in Australian life in the provision of mentoring for young people preparing for work. This is not what employment agencies do, they are concerned primarily with the acquisition of basic skills. A parish which is able to provide work mentors, supporters and encouragers would largely have the field to themselves.

Again, a parish able to sustain and support such a mentoring program for young people would I believe be overwhelmed with candidates. This would be placing your parish at the cutting edge of the most worrying aspect of modern Australian life: getting and holding a job.

Young Men's/Young Women's Groups

There are a large number of specific social and practical skill initiatives that might be undertaken by a passionate parish. Young Australians are not flush with cash, so programs should be as low cost as possible. A full discussion within your parish community could bring up a host of interesting courses that may be offered and sustained by local parishioners, that's the beauty of what you are offering. A practical example of the Christian life with people who live in your area and with whom young people can have an ongoing relationship. There is no point in hiring outsiders to do this heavy lifting, the responsibility lies with parishioners providing you have the skill base necessary. Parishes are often surprised what they have when they ask!

Such initiatives provide excellent ongoing connections with young people in your area and give the parish a connection usually unaffected by university or work commitments. If you have the skill base in your parish, I would strongly recommend contemplating such an initiative, housed on church property. Authentic Mission is not easy, but not enough parishes commit to bold adventures.

(VI) DRUGS

Why

Australian society seems really to have moved to a more permissive attitude to drug use and drug addiction. Of late, a number of State governments have introduced the provision of safe injecting rooms and there is substantial community pressure to allow cannabis usage to be legalised. As it currently stands in most states, those caught in possession of small amounts of cannabis, (if first time offenders) are usually given a caution or a good behaviour bond, without a conviction recorded. Cultivation offences are dealt with more harshly, yet if for personal usage do not normally attract imprisonment. Trafficking offences attract a range of penalties rising to a maximum imprisonment of 15 years for non-commercial quantities. Suppling or selling cannabis to a child, exposes individuals to harsher penalties up to a maximum period of imprisonment of 20 years.

In the last 5-10 years most Australian cities and towns are reporting a significant surge in the usage of Chrystal Methamphetamine, commonly known as "ICE". This drug is a stimulant, in that it speeds up messages between the brain and the body. It is stronger, more harmful and more addictive than the powder forms of Methamphetamines usually known as "SPEED". Most Methamphetamines in Australia are produced locally but large-scale importation has arrived from China and other South East Asian countries. The Australian Federal Police report a significant increase of Mexican Sinaloa Cartel drug importation into Australia since 2017.

In 2018 Australians consumed 9.8 tonnes of Methamphetamine an increase of over one tonne on the previous year. The Australian Criminal Intelligence unit estimates Australia's national spend on this drug to be around 9.3 billion dollars. There is no safe level of drug use for Methamphetamine, overdose is common sometimes resulting in uncontrollable fits, extreme agitation, unconsciousness, stroke, heart attack and death.

A new phenomenon known as ICE psychosis has been noticed in some users and is usually characterised by paranoid delusions, hallucinations and bizarre and aggressive behaviour.

Dependence on ICE can often occur quickly and a strong connection with mental health issues is now commonplace, these may include long term anxiety and depression.

In my view Australian society has a crisis in drug usage at both the allegedly harmless cannabis level and in the aggressive forms of Methamphetamines. Both these drugs are shattering the lives of thousands of Australians. Notwithstanding, the harmless portrayal of marijuana in much of Australia's media and the growing calls in many areas of community life for its legalisation, marijuana does have severe effects on the brain in both the short and long term. In the short-term users often have impaired memory function, difficulties with problem solving, changes in mood, delusions and hallucinations coupled with an increased risk of developing psychosis. In the long term, usage in younger Australians affects brain development and can result in loss of mental abilities, eroding brain connections necessary in learning and memory functions.

Teenagers who use marijuana regularly lose an average of 8 IQ points between the ages of 13 and 38. These mental abilities do not return in those who cease using the drug as adults. Most seriously, long term marijuana use has strong links to the development of mental illness, temporary hallucinations, depression, anxiety and suicidal thoughts.

Compared with those who don't use marijuana, regular users report lower life satisfaction, increased mental health issues, poorer physical health and more frequent relationship problems. There are an increasing number of studies which show alcohol, tobacco and marijuana as "gateway drugs" likely to be used prior to the usage of other drugs.

Much of the thinking of the modern Catholic church has again been formed by the great Pope John Paul II. John Paul pointed out that drugs are one of the main threats facing young people, including children. He suggested that sometimes lack of values or convictions can mean that some young people are easy prey for drug dealers. John Paul II also thought that the decision to take drugs might spring from an ambience of scepticism and hedonism that can lead to feelings of frustration and lack of meaning in people's lives. John Paul II noted that pleasure has a legitimate function in our lives, but that it needs to be ordered so as not to clash with the responsibilities of life, it is the use of our capacities of intelligence and willpower that should regulate our lives.

The church has a vigorous position against illegal drugs, warning potential drug users against using substances that offer the illusion of liberty and false promises of happiness. For John Paul II, the use of drugs is always illicit as it involves an unjustified an irrational abandonment of our capacity to think, choose and act as persons. It is also false to speak of a "right" to drugs, as we never enjoy as humans the right to abdicate personal dignity and responsibility given to us by God. John Paul II rightly notes that using drugs both damages our health and personal capacities but also frustrates our ability to live in community, form partnerships and offer ourselves in service to others.

The church has correctly asserted that combatting the use of drugs is a critical duty for those in political life and other forms of administration and leadership. It is therefore a serious oversight that Australian bishops are utterly absent from "community discussion and engagement".

There is so little offered from the church in Australia that we can only conclude this is not an important issue for the church. Where are the resources for parishes to operate home grown parish initiatives with the aim of strengthening not only those affected within a parish community but also with the life of community in which the parish sits? We should be a key contributor to this debate and follow up with persistent action. Drug addiction destroys lives and Catholicism has a duty to protect individuals and promote the common good. Given the medical and theological knowledge within the church's possession, it must be a more vigorous advocate against the use of drugs.

The wider Australian community seems to be moving towards a separation between "soft" and "hard" drugs, yet behavioural and psychological outcomes don't suggest this separation exists in reality. Both lead to substantial problems, especially in relation to mental health.

There is much the church could do in promoting prevention measures along with support for those with existing problems. The view of the Catholic church cannot sustain a "medicalisation" of the problem, the effects on Catholic families and the wider community demand a "whole church" and wide community advocacy. We should also be more forthright in our support for those policies and other bodies involved in the difficult task of drug prevention and apprehension. Our current understated neglect of this issue both hurts our parish communities and wider society.

Be Local

Every parish within Australia is affected by drugs in some way. In most parish environments it is hidden from view and many parishes will be unaware of any particular circumstances that may be confronting their area. Most police, local government and drug welfare networks will have community outreach workers. Connections with community groups are essential to raising awareness, prevention and therapies to help those already addicted but wanting to make change. Parishes will have to make decisions on the depth of involvement they wish to make. This work can be arduous, of long duration and riddled with failure. This does not make work in your area unachievable and it may be that a focus on education or raising public awareness is a strong first step. In all Authentic Mission activities small steps are important, followed by small measures of success. This builds the necessary confidence to undertake the more complex and demanding mission initiatives. Starting small is the path to success.

What to Do

Education and Prevention Programs

Perhaps the most vital component of drug prevention in Australian society is reducing the demand for drugs, particularly from young Australians. In fact, this is the only way of eradicating this scourge from our society. A parish that undertakes a community outreach program, connecting with local schools, sporting clubs, local businesses and their own primary school is providing a powerful example to the wider community. These initiatives are rarely developed in many communities and certainly not within Australian Catholic parishes.

The dissemination of effective drug information for youth, parents, school groups and local business is effective in raising public awareness of the dangers associated with drugs. Such an initiative is especially important for a number of reasons:

(i) Parents and teenagers need to be aware that brain development is not complete until age 25. In particular, the frontal Cortex which carries out thinking and decision making is not fully developed until that age.

(ii) Statistically we know that when teenagers and young adults acknowledge the physical harm caused by drugs, particularly the strong connection to mental health issues then drug use declines significantly.

(iii) The longer young individuals delay drug usage – addiction and substance disorders are reduced significantly.

Drug Awareness Initiatives in your School

It is never too early to start; increasingly primary

school age children are being exposed to drugs and can gain a false view that drug usage is exciting and not harmful. A consistent set of initiatives designed for specific ages is a valuable tool for hardwiring your school against such views.

If your students have not been exposed to drugs they will soon be. It is often surprising to see that this issue is not tackled in most Catholic primary schools. The parish brings a strong initiative to the school and such work increases the bond between school and parish which are often extremely weak in the Australian context. A parish that is "useful" to its school has a much stronger and natural case for strengthening the bonds between the two in other ways as well.

Organise a Parish Anti-Drug Expo

Such a community-based afternoon or evening is a powerful statement of your parish commitment. There is a lot of work in such an initiative, but it is important you do this on your premises, inviting school groups, councils, police, sporting clubs, rotary, medical professionals – in short, inviting everybody to be part of your initiative. Allowing others to prepare talks, display stalls and distribute information puts your parish at the centre of community action and concern.

This is Catholic mission, we have a strong and important view on the damage that drug use causes, few will be aware of it, but a parish engaging with its community in an area of shared concern is a parish engaged in mission.

Host a Drug Counsellor in your Parish

It may be possible for a parish to host a local drug counsellor on your property for a few hours per week. This may offer opportunities to those within your parish to seek anonymous advice, it may also be an opportunity for the community to offer or strengthen the great gift of the mass and parish community life to someone who is struggling with drugs.

This should not imply the parish is opening itself to drug related trouble or drug paraphernalia on parish grounds. Strong boundaries need to be established, given that schools are often nearby. These are not injecting rooms; they are places of advice and counselling within our Catholic spirituality. There are always some individuals who may mistake the initiative you are offering, yet with the right people involved and clearly stated intentions and rules, such counselling can be a powerful part of your parish network.

Sponsor Drug Education in your Parish and Schools

Many teachers or parish workers often find that they are unsure of the exact facts surrounding drugs in Australia. What are the common drugs? What are their risks? What signs might there be to look out for in individuals? What is the difference between Amphetamines, Benzodiazepines, Depressants and Stimulants? How are they packaged and displayed? This is a huge field and quite confusing for people not directly involved in the day to day drug world.

Nevertheless, this is a valuable exercise for everyone involved in education, youth groups or sporting initiatives. It does send an important message to the wider community and your parish that you are concerned and supportive of the work they undertake within your community.

Anti-Drug Clubs within your School

A combined parish – teacher – student club could be established within your school community to undertake various social, fun-runs, bike-a-thons, essay competitions, all designed to keep the message of the harm of drugs before your school and parish community. Such a club may invite speakers, police or former drug users to engage with the community at school assemblies, special class functions or community fund raisers. The possibility of inviting actors, (or using students) to create role play showing how drugs may be cunningly offered in your area and most importantly the ways students might learn to say no to drug dealers or misguided friends.

Raising Awareness of the Abuse of Prescription Drugs

In the last decade, Australians have become increasingly aware of the hidden dangers of prescription drug usage. In many cases, adult and elderly Australians are also finding risks stemming from overdose and addiction to doctor prescribed medications. A number of commonly prescribed drug, particularly sleeping pills, anti-depressants, painkillers and commonly prescribed Diazepam (Valium) to relieve anxiety are now recognised as causing addiction in large numbers of Australians.

In the case of Valium, addiction can result, if taken for longer than 4-6 weeks. The impact on individual lives can be as pronounced as the consumption of illegal drugs and may result in isolation from family and friends, loss of interest in formerly enjoyable activities and the ignoring of work responsibilities or other commitments.

It may be just as valuable in the parish context to consider additional initiatives, information, or talks in regard to prescription drug usage and possible abuse. It may be possible in your parish to organise and manage a collection and destruction point for unwanted prescription drugs.

In my view issues regarding drugs, their abuse and affects are as vital a concern for "average Australians" as questions of youth unemployment. Both issues affect the future of young Australians but also the health of our community. Catholic parishes that are concerned with changing and developing our society for the better, cannot afford to ignore these issues. Unfortunately, we in the church have been silent for too long.

(VII) THE HEALING PARISH

Why

The majority of Australian Catholics are routinely, suspicious of healing ministries, don't seek them out for themselves or their friends, and commonly connect then "with speaking in tongues" or other strange practices such as "slaying in the spirit". The average Australian parish does not offer an integrated healing ministry connected in any practical way with the sacramental life of the parish.

The daily routine, practice and culture of our Australian parish life doesn't consider such ministry to be essential to parish life nor even a ministry for a "select" group of parishioners. I am also a priest who has not vigorously made any connection with such ministries and the needs of parishioners or wider community aspiration. Australian society shows a good deal of aversion and antipathy to practices considered eccentric or abnormal.

Nevertheless, with these attitudes prominent in our church and the wider community, Catholics are confronted with a significant problem, Jesus himself didn't think or act this way.

> "When the men came to Jesus, they said 'John the Baptist sent us to ask, are you the one who is to come, or should we expect someone else?'

> At the very time Jesus cured many who had diseases, sickness and evil spirits, and gave sight to many who were blind. So he replied to the messenger 'Go back and repeat to John what you have seen and heard': The blind receive sight, the lame walk, those who have leprosy are cleansed, the deaf hear, the dead are raised and the good news is proclaimed to the poor. Blessed is anyone who does not stumble on account of me" (Luke 7. 20-23).

Inescapably, Jesus sees what he does, the healing he performs, the new life he proclaims as intimately connected to who he is, his purpose and the bringing about of the kingdom of God. People noticed that Jesus changed lives and created new worlds.

There is no doubt that the impact and transformation that Jesus enacted are connected to his daily healing activities. Indeed, such healing, he holds as a proof of who he is and the new kingdom unfolding before our eyes. So, what has gone wrong with the Australian church that we no longer really believe this and that our Catholic life and practice is so locked into the secular here and now. No miracles, no daily saints, no passion in our mass, and no ability to transform our world.

The truth of Australian Catholicism is that we are often capable of following and reinforcing the concerns of the secular world. Can we change anything for the oppressed, the sick, the unemployed or the drug afflicted? In our parish life we do little of substance to change our world. Am I too harsh? Yes, probably but what difference do our parishes make to transforming the world? We are in maintenance mode with mergers and slow decline. Perhaps the best example of this is the dramatic erosion of our sacramental life. How few Catholics now see any purpose in reconciliation? Why are we unable to sustain the Catholic life in our schools? Why do so few of thousands confirmed each year, not continue in the faith just a few months later? And why do 80% of young Australians no longer seek the churches sacrament of marriage?

Perhaps, Christ calls us to a new kind of mission and practice built on a counterculture, Authentic and rebellious ministry. We have had no success copying the secular world. The Catechism of the church states strongly:

> "Christs compassion towards the sick and his many healings of every kind are a resplendent sign that 'God has visited his people' and 'the kingdom of God is close at hand.' Jesus had the power not only to heal but to forgive sins, he has come to heal the whole man, soul and body, he is the physician, the sick has need of"
> (Catechism 1503).

Undoubtedly it is time for the Australian Catholic parish to connect with the wider community in new ways. This means we must bring something different to Australian society. The extensive increase in mental health issues, depression, fear, anxiety and inertia is debilitating large numbers in our society.

Could it be of benefit to refocus the sacramental life and discipline of the church to adapt to new forms of mission. This does not require more staff or budget increases but a focus on the mass, that incorporates reconciliation, anointing, the intercession of the saints and the laying on of hands in one continued experience. These are all dimension of parish pastoral care and they should be offered on a wider basis. These are also not just the gifts of one or two individuals but of the "whole body of Christ". It may be possible to offer parish ministry that includes intercession and prayer for the sick before and after the mass. We also need to teach and encourage other parishioners to join with the priest in anointing and laying on of hands. This can be done quietly, subtly and powerfully without disturbance prior to or at the end of mass.

For all those many Australian parishes who have removed statues of our lady and areas to light candles, here is another central ministry in the life of Mary, she comes to comfort those in sorrow and distress. This is not what some have called "old Catholicism" but rather a fresh expression of healing brought to the life of the church.

Many of our Australian parishes are dry and unproductive, we need places where prayer can be ongoing, where our lady is present, where Christ can be seen to minister, where the worried and anxious can encounter Christ. In short, our parish churches need more spaces where ministries, can fruitfully take place, all of which point to the great encounter of meeting Christ in the mass. The Catholic church has always seen the healing encounter with Christ as entirely natural, it is not weird, strange or embarrassing, it is life changing and experiential. If we make our churches placed where people can meet our lady, be anointed, receive prayer, repent of their sins, then new things are possible. The ministry is not ours, it belongs to Christ, but we must open our parish to its fulness.

Be Local

Parishes should certainly consider the formation of 6-8 individuals into a healing group. The responsibility of this group is to pray with the parish priest in a ministry of healing. The primary work of the group is to give reassurance to those in need of healing but who may be hesitate or shy or even a little disbelieving. Christ wills to bring all people to himself, this encounter can be confronting for some, but it is not blocked by cynicism or doubt. We are in the business of transforming the world, offering healing prayer and anointing, to those inside and outside of your parish is a small step in reconciling the world. Be prepared to invite people to come and receive healing prayer. Our secular society is cynical and suspicious of Catholicism so the importance of invitation, its subtleness and gentleness cannot be understated.

What to Do

Make Healing Normal

Healing Ministry does not belong to "born again Christians" or "Charismatic renewal". Healing is part of the normal discipline of the Catholic church. Jesus himself used it as a major dimension of his encounter with the world. He expected transformation, although I'm sure in many cases he didn't witness gratitude and certainly not reward. In the context of Authentic Mission and the world's transformation we also will not often witness gratitude or reward. This work belongs to God, our task is to get on with it. Most parishes will need a period in which healing is "repackaged" as just another normal mission of the church, in the same way we take communion to those at home we also provide a ministry of anointing and healing as part of our normal commitment to the world.

Create a Space in Church where Healing can be Done

Unfortunately, many Australians parishes have removed statues of our lady and areas where candles can be lit. Prayer is not in our churches to be controlled or limited by the priest. I have met many priests who insist that statues and candles belong to a "superstitious past". The re-creation of such spaces is a powerful statement to your parish, and your local community, it means you expect change to happen, lives to be affected and your parish to be a place where your world is changed. If we don't believe this, what on earth are we for? Inertia and hopelessness are in many of our parishes, this is never spoken about, but its signs are unmistakable. In re-creating space for healing, with "real" candles and the presence of our lady and the saints you are clearly stating your hope and expectation of change. Again, if we don't have this belief in the ministry of Christ, what on earth are we for?

Teach and Highlight "Reconciliation" as Central to our Mission

The sacrament of reconciliation is completely ignored and not considered important in many Australian parishes. The sacrament of reconciliation is the great "how am I going sacrament", it is the pre-eminent chance to "touch base with God". It is not about punishment, secrets, embarrassment or anything to be fearful of. In my experience, it will certainly be powerful, sometimes overwhelming, but always about new life and new beginnings.

It is also the base of all healing; it is essentially tied up with new futures and new ways of thinking and being. The practical "message" about reconciliation in most parishes is that it not important and belongs to the past. Nevertheless, as we look at the slow death of many of our parishes, for how long will we see "normal" as doing the same old things.

In the same way as individuals are unable to change until they deal with blockages and barriers to new growth, nor can a parish. Some teaching on the importance of reconciliation to parish life is also crucial. If we don't consider the nature of our life together in reconciliation, how exactly will change happen. If we don't consider what indifference to reconciliation does to our community life as well, are we really serious about transformation. If we won't consider transformation of ourselves, how exactly will we transform the world. Reconciliation as the essential first step in healing, restores the sacrament to its rightful place, not just for the individual but for the parish as well.

Ministry to the Bereaved

Maintaining a ministry to the bereaved is difficult to sustain. Parishes are usually forced to move on quickly as new concerns and pastoral endeavours are never far away. Nonetheless, healing ministry is intimately connected with this group of individuals and families. They are immediately confronted with loss, changed environments and perhaps isolation, of course, out of sight, out of mind is not always the fault of any individuals but it should be guarded against.

It is likely to be the case some parishes consider this to be exclusively the ministry of the priest. Parishes who are seriously considering a focus on healing ministry require a wider group of parishioner to remain in contact with those who grieve over a longer period of time. This should include invitations to services which remember deceased parishioners but also those outside the parish. Healing is about hope and new life, how does this conclude with a funeral? Such a ministry most likely incorporates home visiting, prayers, anointing, invitations to mass and the labour of establishing friendships. This is a "whole" parish exercise and requires a strong connection with a concept of Christs healing impacting on the lives of individuals, families and our world.

Opportunities for a ministry of healing are substantial. They do require thinking about healing in a different way. It is not the precinct of "weird Catholics" but the basis of all ministry. Until healing is habitually seen as a natural part of mass, sacramental life, pastoral care, parish life and caring for each other, we are likely to continue in parish expressions that still seem to be unable to change and make no difference to our world.

The confronting words of Jesus, post his resurrection, are perhaps more astonishing to the Australian church than ever before.

"Therefore, go and make disciples of all nations, baptising the in the name of the Father and of the Son and of the Holy Spirit and teaching them to obey everything I have commanded you. And surely, I am with you always, to the very end of the age" (Matthew 28. 19-20).

(VIII) AFFIRM THE MARTYRS

At the centre of Australian Catholicism's lack of mission is an absence of honour and appreciation for the martyrs of the church. The word "martyr" itself means witness. The fundamental action of the martyr is to be a witness to the person of Christ. A witness, even to the point of death, but the emphasis is not on death, it is on the centrality of witness.

What is uniquely characteristic of the martyr is the overcoming of fear, which allows the martyr to speak to his society, to speak to the powerful without compromise and without conforming to the powers of the day. Therein lies the problem for Australian Catholics. We have no martyrs, that is why we have so few people prepared to speak out against the wrong headiness of government or a society so permissive that the destruction of alcohol, drugs, broken relationships, fragment families and depressed individuals continue to grow each day and each year.

We are a church so fearful of our circumstances that the Victorian State Government has within the last ten years passed legislation making voluntary euthanasia legal (2019), abortion beyond 24 weeks with the agreement of 2 medical practitioners (2008) and Priests in Victoria and Tasmania now facing jail terms if they do not report information regarding child sexual abuse made during the sacrament of confession

(2019). Whatever an individual's private view on these matters, it is now undeniable that State governments are emboldened to encroach on sacramental life and largely ignore Catholic viewpoints on the beginning and end of life ethics.

The initial church response has been severely muted, and no follow up campaigns, advertising or demonstrations have ensued. Our fear that government funding of Catholic hospitals and schools may be reduced is palpable. The Catholic church throughout history has resisted state attempts to subordinate the church to itself. The martyrs, St Thomas More and St John Fisher attest to this, but where is the response of Australian Catholics?

The Australian Catholic church also has an alarming lack of insight into what persecution really means. Primarily, persecution is designed to silence the ability to witness and proclaim the life of Christ. In many parts of the world, Catholics live each day in fear of arrest, torture, denial of basic rights to education and housing but how do Australian Catholics respond – complete silence. Silence is our basic modus operandi Australian Catholics are at great risk of the condemnation of Christ who exalted and dignified, those who live the beatitudes.

> "Blessed are those who are persecuted because of righteousness, for theirs is the Kingdom of heaven. Blessed are you when people insult you, persecute you and falsely say all kinds of evil

against you because of me. Rejoice and be glad, because great is your reward in heaven, for in the same way they persecuted the prophets who were before you" (Matthew 5. 1-12).

Of course, in Australian Catholic life these verses only apply to somebody else.

Australian Catholics are being called to consider the lives and deaths of those around the world, who witness for Christ. Their witness should motivate us to take our faith more seriously. In recent history we have many examples, in World War II, Bernard Lichtenberg and Max Kolbe, under communist rule, John Paul II and Jerzy Popieluszko, these are but a few of those who witnessed without fear. As Australian Catholics we also have a calling and a choice to stand against wrong and affirm the life of Christ. Affirming the martyr's is the vital first step.

Be Local

Australian Catholic parishes are called to live parish life in solidarity with others. We witness and speak out on behalf of others. We are not a private club for selected members, rather we are the body of Christ, which takes action and seeks to change the world. What does this really mean? It means that we should not allow injustices to take place without consequence or in silence, be they, in Australia or anywhere else.

The situation of the early church was always precarious and unstable, that is the nature of the church. Opponents of the early church were forced to invent new laws, in an effort to silence Christians. The historian Tacitus notes that Christians under Nero were simply charged with "hatred of humanity", execution followed quickly. The process of inventing and subverting laws to silence Catholics is not new, Victorian state laws are just another example.

Interestingly, Roman society in practice was not too different to our own. Divorce was easy, abortion normal, drunkenness common, assaults after dark frequent. It may be that our secular form of Government is also similar in its demands for Catholics to silence their belief in human dignity, the right to life and their freedom to speak of Christ's importance in their life.

Australian parishes need to consider again, how to fearlessly talk about Christ in our areas, what can we invite community members to? Do we still run fetes? Do we have tours of our churches? Do we produce material to describe our life together? Do we letter box drop for our feast days? Have we a stand-alone website noting our beliefs and parish life together? Are we advocating in our community for right to life and end of life ethics, or the beauty of marriage? Many of these basic activities and connections have been removed from parish life... Why? Is it somehow too hard or are we afraid of what others might think? Australian society needs our voice, competing, arguing and advocating. Silence is not an option; the worldwide martyred church demands that it not be.

What to Do

Place pictures of martyrs in your church

Parishioners need to see and know a little of the story of martyr's in our Catholic life, particularly, we need to hear of the lives of modern martyrs. The martyr's often can be remembered within the particular persecution or fear they confronted and resisted. Catholicism is always a faith that is called to contend with and stand-up to the world, this is how we bring about the fulfilment of Christ's mission to all creation. When we highlight the forms of persecution the church has resisted, we note to our own parishioners, that things will be no different from us.

Perhaps displays could be staged in different parts of the church or church foyers, featuring, Catholic resistance to National Socialism (Kolbe, Lichtenberg) or communism (John Paul II, Popieluszko, Mindszenty) or the Christian martyrs under Islam (Roderick and the Cordova martyrs) or modern-day persecution in Syria under ISIS. We should also highlight the martyrs of alleged secular enlightenment notably during the French revolution and reign of terror (the Carmelites of Compiegne). The seizing of the Cathedral of Notre Dame repurposed as a temple to the Goddess Reason, specially hosting a prostitute on the altar and dedicated to lurid behaviours. It may be the case in Australia that we are again witnessing the dreams of the secular state, which often talk of peace and liberty, but often deliver restrictions and oppression, not only to Catholics but usually starting with them.

Displays of Martyrs in your Schools

Our Catholic education system is critically missing knowledge of our Catholic history. This includes not only our beliefs which are thinly taught but also of our world-wide history, particularly the things we have fought against and why. This is a clear-cut opportunity to talk about the beliefs of Catholicism and the beauty of the Catholic martyrs. These are not hardened and stilted individuals but overwhelming gracious and respectful despite persecution, yet primarily determined to serve Christ first. Perhaps this is summed up best by St Thomas more, who said on the scaffold "I die the king's faithful servant, but God's first." The martyrs are an ideal example of Catholicism to be promoting to young Catholics.

Parishioners Speaking in School about their Favourite Martyr

The connection between parish and school in the Australian context are often thin. It may well be possible for motivated parishioners to undertake some classroom or assembly presentation in your local school. This could help to strengthen or re-activate the connection between school and parish.

The importance of such connections cannot be overstated. The situation for Australian Catholics is not yet one of full-blown martyrdom, yet the church is often ridiculed for her teachings on traditional marriage, defence of the unborn and her concerns regarding doctor assisted suicide. Increasingly, Catholics are told your viewpoints are not welcome here or we do not have a platform for you to speak.

Australian Catholics must end their long silence. We must begin to speak the truth to all Australians, we are called to be witnesses to the life and person of Jesus. This means we will be uninvited, often ignored and sometimes persecuted. Perhaps the letter to the Hebrews sums up the situation of Australian Catholics.

> "Consider him who endured such opposition from sinners, so that you will not grow weary and lose heart. In your struggle against sin, you have not yet resisted to the point of shedding your blood" (Hebrew 12, 3-4).

(IX) SUPPORT PERSECUTED CHRISTIANS

The twentieth century and early twenty-first century has seen the greatest levels of Christian/Catholic persecution in our 2000-year history. This persecution has been so severe that we are witnessing the end of Christian culture and residence in many countries. Death and destruction has been so severe that in some nations, the passing on of the faith to the next generation has become unlikely, there are not enough young Christians to ensure its survival. It is a serious scandal, and a prodigious stain on the Catholic leadership of Australia that we have hardly mentioned this to our parishes, to our politicians, to our schools, to our wider communities. We have not even conducted a miniscule media or advocacy campaign. There is no excuse.

Unfortunately, our indifference to our Catholic brothers and sisters throughout the world is a key reason why we are unsuccessful with mission to our fellow Australians. We are a church totally distracted by the concerns of the secular world, so our religious focus is also on agenda's in relation to carbon emissions, climate change or politically correct speech. We are a nation immersed in trivia and Australian Catholicism has sunk into a black hole of undervalued life and shrunken messages. What on earth does Australian Catholicism stand for?

When we cannot stand up for persecuted brother and sisters, what of meaning can we say to idle and vacuous Australia? The formation of an advocacy group of persecuted Catholics and other Christians is an important measure for changing the psychology of your parish to being one of gravitas, purpose and future. Perhaps, when we can reach this point, some will consider joining us as well!

There are a great many sources of Catholic persecution. Many Catholics mistakenly believe that communist and extreme socialist regimes no longer carry out persecution on Catholics or other Christians. This is not correct and nations such as Cuba, China, Vietnam, Laos and North Korea, all have extensive and active persecution against Christians. This often takes the form of arrest, torture, travel bans and surveillance on family members and friends. For communist regimes, Catholicism is still their number one enemy, as belief in God challenges a fundamental tenet of communists: that mankind is the supreme arbiter of human interactions. No communist regime in history has not persecuted Christians and such persecution is practised extensively in countries that claim this philosophy today.

Unfortunately, the desire for fruitful interfaith dialogue can mask the reality of what happens on the ground, in the day to day life of Christians living within Islamic regimes. Intolerance, bans on church building, job discrimination and the abduction and forced rape and marriage of Christian girls is common and rising in some countries. Egypt, Pakistan, Saudi Arabia, Iran, Iraq, Somalia, Afghanistan, Sudan, Libya, Yemen and Indonesia still have extensive persecution as the natural experience of Christians. It is both the case that governments are involved in the active persecution of Christians, especially through building restrictions on churches, travel bans for Catholic priests and the denial of secondary and university education. Additionally, these governments are slow to respond to acts of violence committed against Christians, police often do not attend incidents involving Christians or when Christian property is vandalised or destroyed.

The Australian government and the Australian Catholic church make few diplomatic efforts to highlight or sanction such behaviour. The legitimate concern and desire to help Christians in Islamic nations does not imply the church is targeting Islam or lacking some kind of respect for Australian Muslims. The situation for most Catholics in Islamic nations is grave, but on what grounds can we continue to ignore such treatment of our brothers and sisters in Christ?

Recent surveys of Catholics in the U.S.A has revealed a dramatic rise in concern of persecuted Christians. 58% of U.S Catholics said persecution was the gravest problem facing the church, rated as more concerning than climate change (CNS survey, March 2019). Only 19% said their parish was engaged with the issue, only 25% found that bishops sufficiently engaged and only 50% thought Pope Francis was doing enough.

Respondents to the survey were particularly keen to see an increase in policy interventions. 61% saw diplomatic pressure as important, 56% thought economic sanctions of some value and 53% thought emergency asylum as a relevant response. Sadly, the concerns of Australian Catholics have never been surveyed. Pope John Paul II's teaching on the martyrs of our century is an excellent place to consider the response that we as Catholics should be making. Nevertheless, the sad reality of the early twentieth century is that nothing has changed.

Be Local

Christian persecution is so rarely spoken about in Australia that most of our fellow Australians will not be aware that it is taking place on a global front. We have so little skin in the game that many Catholics themselves will know nothing of the issue.

It is unlikely that many networks will be available for you to join within Australian Catholicism, much of this work will need to begin with you. Aid to the church in need (Australia) does have some resource that can be purchased. These videos and piety resources are a valuable beginning to understanding Catholic and other Christian persecution yet, they are not fundamentally an advocacy or parish-based network.

This is what the Australian church needs, passionate, undeterred and vibrant individuals in local areas prepared to stand up for Christians living in the wilderness.

If we are only Catholic's responding to a Jesus who brings us light, joy, peace and comfort, but we know nothing of the evil confronting Catholics in the wider world, then in what ways are we really Catholic?

What to Do

Create your Own Inter-Parish Network

A few passionate individuals can make an enormous difference. It could well be possible with 6-8 parishes joining together to do some significant fund-raising or some substantial lobbying of local politicians. Fund raising to help in the creation of a Christian school overseas or the construction of one part of a parish can be surprisingly cheap. Serious issues can arrive in relation to corruption and trust in some countries but if you can discover a connection in a Catholic area then good things can be achieved. You do not need to be committing huge sums to make a difference. Trusted connections in a host parish are the key. The Sudanese, Nigerian and Indian churches are all looking for partners. It is long and hard work, but great rewards are possible.

Talk to your School

Establish a number of parishioners who are willing to talk and provide material about what is happening in the wider church. Australian children need reasons to be proud of Catholicism and examples of people building their faith in the face of great odds. Your school might also consider how it might support ongoing awareness of these Christians within your school.

It is also an important message to Australian Catholic students, that the obstacles and expression of persecuted Catholics may give local Australian children, beginning in the faith a model on how to live Catholicism in an effective way. Australian Catholicism provides virtually no models for how to be a Catholic in the wider world, yet the tribulation and examples of what others can undertake and endure for their faith, could set current models for our own students. So many of our own young Catholics fall away at the first sign of peer pressure and models of stronger and enduring individuals can only be helpful.

Write to overseas Ambassadors and lobby your Federal and State Members

Catholics often seem to consider lobbying to be an ineffective undertaking, possibly this is also linked to a desire not to upset State Governments, given that Catholics schools receive substantial government funding. It is disappointing that we can be aroused into advocacy when we perceive this funding might be reduced, but that we are stimulated to do so little on other anti-Catholic causes.

Persecution of our fellow Catholics and Christians worldwide is an attack on our faith and moral understanding as well. Advocating for Catholic cause goes to the heart of the way we choose to live our faith. If Catholicism is to be a nice, pleasant, club like, add on to our lives, then we are unlikely to achieve much for the wider faith. Sadly, our local expression of the faith is eroded constantly, because we are unable to see and understand a Catholicism beyond our own local expression.

This pleasant, club like Catholicism cannot change the world and there is now significant evidence that it is not allowing us to grow or stand up for ourselves in the Australian context either.

Advocating for persecuted Catholics, says a lot about who we are as Australian Catholics. When we write to ambassadors and do so until they respond, when we write to our politicians about our concerns, when we are prepared to send delegations to meet, when we letterbox our local area, we are doing much more than drawing attention to the difficulties of Catholics in faraway places – we are making a statement about our own life, values and place in our communities. If our society never hears from you as a parish, or continues to feel so comfortable in ignoring the church and its politically correct bishops, then how is Australian Catholicism actually living the faith? When we consider persecuted overseas Catholics, we consider our own position as well.

Support a Parish Overseas

It would take a determined effort to connect directly with an overseas parish suffering persecution. To make this successfully work you need person to person relationships. It is always unsafe to deposit money into unknown overseas accounts, but it is possible, (having done it myself) to bring financial support to a parish physically. This means the possibility of parishioners, (or organised groups) travelling to your adopted parish, to see and understand concrete realities on the ground. This is a huge commitment from your parish, but it can be done, yet the commitment is an even greater benefit to the receiving community. Usually, your commitment would need to be for around 5 years, anything less does not really allow significant growth to occur. Many countries are physically dangerous, but it is the case that safer options are available still in Vietnam, India and Indonesia. In the end the outcomes depend on trust, yet this is the basis of all human interactions anyway. Good results can work with good partners and sensitivity to local conditions.

Badger your Bishop

It may be possible to consider a more extensive project, if a number of parishes are prepared to work together, using the contacts of your local diocese or archdiocese. If you wish your project to finish at this stage hand control over to them! I am suggesting using whatever networks may be available to develop and strengthen your own local networks. Like all undertakings Authentic Mission is local and any work you consider with persecuted Christians will still be dependent on the energy, drive and purpose of your local network of interested parishioners.

This situation of the persecuted church is worse than at any time since the death and resurrection of our Lord. The call to Australian Catholics cannot be one that is only concerned with our needs and our hopes. Such a call is not an authentic Catholic one. In finding a voice for persecuted Catholics we may discover a more vigorous one for ourselves.

AUTHENTIC MISSION: IN DEPTH

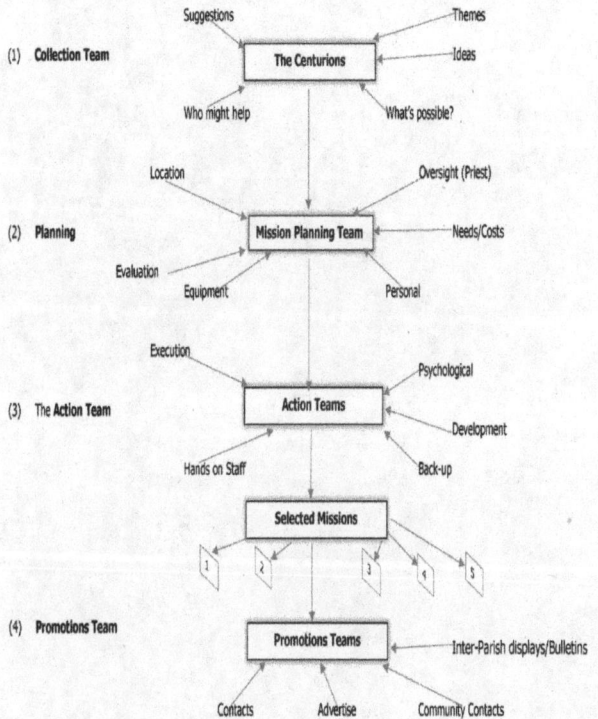

www.ingramcontent.com/pod-product-compliance
Lightning Source LLC
Chambersburg PA
CBHW011954150426
43199CB00019B/2865